ST. PAUL

ST. PAUL

ARTHUR DARBY NOCK

*Frothingham Professor of the History
of Religion in Harvard University;
Corresponding Member of the Berlin
Academy of Sciences; Foreign Member
of the Royal Society of Letters of
Lund; Corresponding Fellow of the
British Academy.*

HARPER AND BROTHERS

NEW YORK

PRINTED IN THE UNITED STATES OF AMERICA

To

WILLARD AND MURIEL SPERRY

CONTENTS

FOREWORD

THE life work of St. Paul has exercised a profound influence on more than eighteen centuries, and his writings and thought have been subjected to the closest scrutiny by many generations of serious workers. No individual can do justice to the complexity of issues which are involved. If this small book makes it easier for any readers to see St. Paul as a man and as a writer in the context of his times, I shall be more than content.

My best thanks are due to the Theological Seminary of the Reformed Church in the United States at Lancaster, Pennsylvania, where the substance of this work was delivered on the Swander lectureship, to its President, Dr. George W. Richards, and further to Canon J. M. Creed, Professor C. H. Dodd, and Mr. M. P. Charlesworth for their friendly aid.

ARTHUR DARBY NOCK.

HARVARD UNIVERSITY,
    CAMBRIDGE, MASSACHUSETTS.
December 9, 1937.

CHAPTER I

INTRODUCTION

A STUDENT who wishes to know about St. Paul may at the beginning think that he is in a very fortunate position. We possess from St. Paul's hand a number of writings of undoubted authenticity : the two Epistles to the Thessalonians ; the two Epistles to the Corinthians ; the Epistle to the Galatians ; the Epistle to the Romans ; the Epistles to the Philippians, the Colossians, and Philemon. (The letter which is called the Epistle to the Ephesians must be omitted, as probably of the next generation, although the thoughts it expresses may fairly be regarded as derived from Paul and not inconsistent with his own thinking : the so-called Pastoral Epistles—that is to say the two letters to Timothy and the letter to Titus— belonging as they must do to a subsequent period, contain nevertheless information which may be genuine, if not fragments which may be authentic.) These letters we possess in a text which is of remarkable trustworthiness. Naturally we have reason to suspect occasional interpolations : and the present shape of the Second Epistle to the

11

Corinthians is almost certainly due to the editorial putting together of material which is all Pauline but which was written on different occasions. Attempts have been made to show that the text has been freely rehandled in the interest of later presuppositions and it is easy to point to inconsistencies : but Paul does not seem to have sought consistency. For most scholars the coherence and individuality, both of style and of ideas, and in particular of ideas which in later times became largely unintelligible because their setting was lost and for Christians the battle had shifted to other fields, will be decisive against any such suppositions. Probability is the guide of life.

We have not only this body of writings by Paul himself ; we have also in the Acts of the Apostles a record which, if not, as tradition asserts, written entirely by one who shared many of his travels, does at least, almost beyond doubt, include material taken from the diary of that fellow-traveller. This account shows at every point a remarkable sense for concrete situations and a notable accuracy in certain details of contemporary life which can be verified from the documentary and archaeological remains of the ancient world. We have then these materials, and it might seem that we were in a very favourable position for their interpretation.

After all, Paul was by birth a Jew, and the Jewish religion is known to us from a chain of sources which range over many centuries. He spoke Greek and his thinking was coloured by his speaking of Greek; and the thought of the Greeks is not only something which we can study but also an integral part of our culture and of our general ideas. He became a Christian, and Christianity in some form or other is for nearly all of us a phenomenon with which we have been familiar from early years.

Nevertheless, the moment we look into these things a little more closely, we begin to discover difficulties of a very grave kind. The Pauline Epistles are extraordinarily difficult to interpret. Read in English, in the light of Scripture teaching and sermons in church, they have a certain deceptive familiarity and naturalness, although, to be sure, it is a fair question how many of those who have attended the Anglican burial service can attach much meaning to the prescribed reading from 1 Cor. xv. If we approach these letters in the original Greek, and come to them from the reading of other Greek texts of the period, there is not a paragraph which does not pull us up with a start as containing something which is, from that standpoint, barely intelligible. All translation is to some extent interpretation; and such interpretation is dangerous when applied to Paul, who freely used words admitting of an extended range of meaning. Furthermore, the Pauline Epistles were not written in a restful, reflective mood. They contain nothing which corresponds to a *Summa*

Theologica. The Epistle to the Romans indeed comes nearest to this, for the reason that in it Paul was trying to make as attractive a presentation as he could of his own point of view to a Christian community to which he was personally unknown. The other Epistles, apart from the brief note to Philemon on a private matter, are all products of the emotions and the controversies of individual moments and situations. In them Paul is making the written word serve as a substitute for direct speech. He writes to the Corinthians, he writes to the Galatians in the agony of heart which comes of the feeling that his work in Christ is being undone by false teachers, factious rivalries, and a mixture of stupidity and vice. His words sometimes tumble over one another ; there are the brief, vivid violences which most men would, on later reflection, have removed. Above all, there is a constant allusiveness ; and what is common ground between him and his adversaries, or between him and his forgetful and disloyal pupils, is taken for granted. That is not all : the Pauline Epistles give us no clue to the early shaping of Paul's thought. They fall between A.D. 50 and at very latest A.D. 64. The First Epistle to the Thessalonians, which is probably the oldest of them, comes from a time when Paul had been a Christian not less than seventeen years, possibly longer, and when his serious clash with the Church of Jerusalem lay behind him. We see in these Epistles features of development, but the main story is earlier.

When we turn from the Epistles to the Acts, we encounter difficulties which are no less grave. The narrative has an appearance of continuity and of simple clarity and sincerity, but when we try to bring it into relation with Paul's own writings, we at once find grave inconsistencies. Above all, the story of the Apostolic Council at Jerusalem in Acts xv. cannot be reconciled with the autobiographical fragment in Galatians ii. except by critical hypotheses which are highly detrimental to the historical precision of Acts (pp. 116–117, later). Moreover, Acts does not tell a continuous story : Paul spent two years and three months at Ephesus, but the narrative records only certain striking episodes. Excellent materials and in particular the ' We source ' are combined with less good materials by rapid transitions. Further, the writer of Acts lived in a time in which the controversial issues of Paul's life had faded into obscurity and become unintelligible.

Again, we are under great disadvantages in studying the Judaism in which Paul grew up. We have on the one hand the Old Testament, the latest book of which is Daniel (between 168 and 165 B.C.). On the other hand, we have our evidence for the orthodox Judaism which found classic expression from the second century of our era onwards. The great Pharisee teachers of the first century were probably not far from it in spirit, but only isolated sayings survive with their names, and many issues, later closed, were open in their days. A time of vigorous and highly diverse development lies between the time of Daniel and the second century of our era.

Two of its aspects, Apocalyptic and Hellenization, are well represented in extant literature, and the survival of that literature is in each case due to Christians and not to Jews. The writings of the first have been discussed in this series by the late R. H. Charles in his volume, *Religious Development between the Old and New Testaments* ; they belong to a Palestinian literature which describes the various forms in which pious Jews expected the hope of Israel to be fulfilled in the Sovereignty of God, which was often thought to be brought in by the rule of his Anointed Servant, the Messiah. The hope remained, but without its old immediacy, and the literature was discarded. The Hellenistic interpretation of Judaism, on the other hand, was not primarily concerned with the hope of such a consummation, but rather regarded the inspired literature of the Old Testament, and above all the Law, that is to say the Pentateuch, as an expression in figurative terms of the highest wisdom which mankind could conceive, a revelation therefore in which the best insights of Plato and Aristotle and the Stoics must necessarily be subsumed. Paul himself speaks of the Jew (Rom. ii. 19) as confident of being ' a guide of the blind . . . having the conformation of knowledge and truth in the Law '. This type of thought is known to us from Philo, a Jew of Alexandria who wrote in the first half of the first century of our era. Like many expressions of Jewish Apocalyptic, it was later rejected by the religious consciousness of the nation, which retained religious universalism but in a somewhat theoretical way.

Palestinian Judaism included a wide range of diverse opinion. The Pharisees attached extreme importance to that oral tradition which had grown up in centuries of meditation by pious men on God's commandments, believed in the after-life, and held as an ideal the hope of perfecting Israel in the observation of the divine code ; they looked to the acknowledgment of God's Sovereignty in this way as also to its realization by divine action as foretold in prophecy and Apocalyptic. Their ideal was personal holiness within a holy nation. Pharisaism was the basis of later standard Judaism. They were an influential and respected party ; but much influence rested with the Sadducees who held to the letter of the law, rejected the after-life, other Pharisaic interpretations, and anything which savoured of theological modernism, and concerned themselves with the good order of the Temple and its worship as established. Later their name became a name of heresy. We hear at this time also of the Essenes, who lived as an ascetic confraternity in the desert, rejecting marriage, eschewing private property, and finding their religious satisfaction in a communal life. There were individual hermits, like that Bannus with whom the historian Josephus says he spent three years, and the political revolutionaries, who sought to bring in God's Sovereignty by violent action. Nor must we forget the much larger numbers of ordinary people, loyal to the Judaism in which they were reared, loyal according to their lights but unversed in the subtleties of religious parties. There was not a little confusion of what we should call nationalism, with what we should call religion—things which for a Jew could not be kept apart, since the essential points of Jewish faith were the Law, the People, and the Temple. If for Jesus the kingdom was not of this world, it was otherwise for them ; any place for the heathen which might be in it would be a place of penitence and tears.

There were further differences between the Judaism of Palestine and the Judaism of the Jews, several times as numerous, who were scattered over the rest of the civilized world of the time. But even in Palestine there was a great range of difference, and unfortunately we have little evidence which enables us to interpret this correctly except the Apocalyptic works which the Christians preserved, the New Testament, which gives necessarily partisan accounts of various kinds, and the historian Josephus who wrote at Rome between

A.D. 75 and 96 with his eye on the world outside : he could have told us so much. We have, therefore, no small difficulty in putting the constituent elements of the Judaism contemporary with Jesus and with Paul into anything like a proper perspective.

Again, we know indeed that Paul was converted to Christianity, but we are imperfectly acquainted with the form which Christianity had taken at the time when Paul became a Christian. His conversion lies at a point between eighteen months and five years after the death of Jesus, and his writings are certainly earlier than our Gospels. Paul came into the Christian Movement when it was gradually finding its feet as a special form of piety within Judaism ; he was dead before the final break with Judaism. Again, while we have a large mass of material in relation to the culture of the Greek world in general under the Roman Empire, that material is far less copious for the first half of the first century than it is for the second century of our era, and while for much we can safely make inferences backwards, there remains a considerable margin of error in them.

There are these initial difficulties in any serious study of Paul. They are not the only difficulties. The words and concepts with which Paul faced the situations of his life and mission have become charged with the dogmatic controversies of later generations. In particular, the significance which some of his writings (and above all the Epistle to the Romans) had for Martin Luther, causes us to read some of his work with later issues near the surface of our minds. That is no unique phenomenon. One of the signs of great religious thought and great religious literature is that both of them are capable of bearing so many meanings which were not in the minds of their authors. Succeeding generations have read the Psalms and have found in them a quintessence of piety without being concerned with the precise significance and contexts in which, over centuries, these poems were written. The works of Plato became of religious significance when they were read five centuries after his death in a sense largely different from that which he had probably put upon them. So it is with Paul. We shall not here concern ourselves with these later interpretations; we shall try to forget for the moment all that happened after his execution at Rome, and, instead, seek as far as we can to view Paul as a man of the first century, living and moving and teaching in its peculiar conditions. For reasons which have been stated, the work of reconstruction cannot be complete : but it yields a picture which in its broader aspects must correspond fairly well to the reality.

CHAPTER II

TARSUS AND JERUSALEM

PAUL was born at Tarsus in Cilicia. He had
the Jewish name Saul as well as the Gentile name
Paul, and was sprung of purely Jewish stock, ' of
the tribe of Benjamin ' (Phil. iii. 5 ; Rom. xi. 1) :
Acts xxiii. 16 speaks of a sister's son as living in
Jerusalem and able to learn of a Jewish plot—
probably therefore not a Christian. Jerome, writing
in the fourth century of our era, preserves a tradition that his family came from Gischala in Galilee.
Be this as it may—and if that is its origin, it was
probably an ultimate and not an immediate origin
—his father acquired Roman citizenship, whether
as a reward for services to some Roman functionary
or through manumission at Rome after being sold
as a slave and then freed, we do not know. His
family was presumably one of wealth and standing.
He learned the craft of a tent-maker,[1] but a student
of the Law always had a trade by which he could
live : it does not prove poverty, and as C. H. Dodd
remarks apropos of 1 Cor. iv. 12, ' A man born

[1] Latin versions give ' leather-worker ' : but *skenopoios*
could hardly mean that.

to manual labour does not speak self-consciously
of " labouring with my own hands ".'

Paul was born in a city which Acts represents
him as calling ' not undistinguished '.[1] It had a
long history of culture ; it had seen the power of
the Hittites ; it had been the centre of government
of a Persian satrapy (which corresponded, broadly
speaking, to a Roman province), and it had remained an important city during the Hellenistic
period. Tarsus had a considerable reputation for
culture ; we know of several Stoic philosophers
who were born there, including Athenodorus who
was a confidant of the Emperor Augustus ; and
the contemporary geographer Strabo says (p. 673)
that the people at Tarsus devoted themselves so
eagerly, not only to philosophy, but also to general
education, that they surpassed Athens, Alexandria,
and any other place where philosophers taught :
the peculiarity of Tarsus was that there the lovers
of learning were all natives. Yet the Tarsians
went abroad to complete their mental training :
' they like to live abroad, and few return '. Later
writers give accounts which, while less glowing,
indicate that Tarsus made considerable claims.

Like many other cities of Asia Minor, it had a
Jewish colony which preserved the customs of the

---

[1] Acts xxi. 39, where he calls himself a citizen ; but
as a Jew he had at most the right of becoming a citizen
if he apostatized (W. W. Tarn, *Hellenistic Civilization*,
ed. 2, pp. 192 f.).

fathers and sent annually to the Temple at Jerusalem the tax of two drachmae to which every male
Jew twenty years of age and more outside of
Judaea was liable. For such Jews the religious
centre of life was to be found in their synagogues.
The synagogue, a religious institution the exact
origin of which we cannot date, is essentially a
meeting; ten male Jews could constitute one.
This meeting had its Sabbath service which began
with the old form (Deut. vi. 4 f.) : ' Hear, O Israel,
the Lord our God, the Lord is One, and thou
shalt love the Lord thy God with all thy heart,
and with all thy soul, and with all thy might,' and
continued with prayer and the reading, commonly
in Greek in the Dispersion, of portions of the Law
and of the Prophets, first in Hebrew and then in
an oral translation (at Alexandria, and perhaps
elsewhere, the written Greek translation which we
know as the Septuagint was no doubt used), and
a sermon. This type of service is familiar to us
to-day as the main pattern of Protestant as well
as of Mohammedan worship. It came to bulk
larger and larger in Jewish religious life. While
any Jew of priestly descent probably had then, as
later, privileges in the synagogal worship, that worship was in no sense dependent on the priestly
caste. It was customary, wherever possible, to
have as many as seven individuals in the congregation take part in the reading of God's Word, and
the sermon was assigned to any competent indi-

vidual in the congregation. So it is that we read in the New Testament of Jesus and of Paul addressing the gathering. The synagogue had its administrative officers ; but it had no priesthood. The complement of the synagogue was the school in which young Jews learned the customs and the sacred language of their fathers. The survival of Judaism through the long centuries of oppression is mainly due to the synagogue. Its prayers preserved the religious genius of the Prophets and the Psalms. The nation as a whole was thus educated in its religious traditions and its instincts were reinforced by the methodical study of the Law. ' My delight is in thy statutes, O Lord.'

The young Paul grew up in the circle of this piety. He would learn from early years that God had chosen Abraham, the man he loved, and brought him forth from his original home ; that Abraham was the father of the nation of Israel to which God had given his promises and which was his chosen people ; that God had raised up Moses as his Lawgiver and made the second promise of the Covenant of Sinai to them ; that he had not only brought them out of their bitter captivity in the land of Egypt and spoiled the spoilers, but had also shown to them, in the revelation of the Law, the ways of his own household in which they, as his family, were to walk ; that he had bestowed upon them the good land of Palestine, defeating for them all the heathen nations which had sought to bar their way ; that he had given to them the King David who took Jerusalem and made it God's Holy City, where Solomon built that Temple in which God's eyes and heart should abide for ever ; that for the sins of the people he had chastised them with deportation and exile ; that he had then restored a faithful remnant to their native land. Paul must needs hear also of that last drastic clash of Jewish piety represented by the Maccabees and Greek culture represented by Antiochus, which is the point from which serious animosities between Jew and non-Jew take their increase ; of God's deliverance of his people ; of the new Jewish monarchy which followed, and of its tragic failure through human sin ; of the humiliation which followed when Pompey entered Jerusalem in 63 B.C.

Paul would hear also of the Hope of Israel ; he would receive the dream that God would raise up an Anointed King of the line of David who should purify Jerusalem of all aliens, and subdue the peoples of the world under the authority of God, and introduce the Good Times. He would learn also of the emphasis which the Pharisees placed on the most minute observation of God's commands and of the hope that if those commands should be fulfilled by all Israel, even for a day, God would at once bring in the Kingdom. He would share the dream of the time when the scattered folk of Israel should be gathered from the four quarters of the world into Palestine. He might be encouraged to think that this dream—in this or in a less nationalistic shape—was near its fulfilment.

Paul would also learn something about the world outside. We can form some picture of the type of teaching which he would receive if we look at the literature written by Jews in the last two centuries before Christ, and notably at the book which is known as the Wisdom of Solomon. The heathen had rejected God's truth and had made images which, although patently composed of inanimate matter, they persisted in worshipping as though divine. He would learn also that these same Gentiles were prone to every kind of vice, to murder, to sexual offences, to lawlessness; they were more remote from him than he was from them. At the same time Paul would be aware that some who were not Jews by birth had become Jews by adoption, or as we might say by naturalization; that is the meaning of the term 'proselyte'. The proselyte was a Gentile who, by the threefold ceremony of circumcision, immersion in water, and (ideally) an offering in the Temple, had come under the shelter of the Jewish name and accepted those obligations which were not only the duty but also the peculiar privilege of Israel. Paul may also in early years have become aware of the existence in the synagogue of persons who, while not becoming proselytes, nevertheless attended the services of the synagogue and kept a minimal standard of conduct which was held to be binding on all mankind. Further, he could hardly fail to hear of philosophy as a pagan activity much of which was compatible with Jewish loyalty and some of which could be pressed into the service of the Jewish religion for its interpretation and defence. The Wisdom of Solomon is one of a chain of testimonies for such adaptation : we cannot believe that the sermons in the Tarsus synagogues were uniformly free from it.

Paul must also have learned in childhood the use of the Greek language. His writings show that he acquired a real mastery of it and had an ear for rhythm, but they are marked by an extreme rarity of echoes from the classical writers and the constant presence of words and phrases from the Septuagint, and lack the merits and demerits alike of the Greek schools of eloquence (p. 234, later). We may reasonably suppose that Paul learned his Greek in a Jewish environment,[1] and a Jewish environment which was more Jewish and less Hellenic than the schools of Alexandria. Philo would have been as much pained by Paul's style as by Paul's thought. Whereas Philo and many Hellenistic Jews in a measure superimposed the Greek cultural and philosophic concept of universalism on their Jewish faith and nationalism, Paul's universalism was a necessary inference from the one-

[1] It is not likely that his parents would have allowed him to frequent a pagan school.

ness of God (Rom. iii. 29 f.) and from the fact of
Christ as he came to conceive it: we may go further
and say, an unwilling inference. Men became
equal ' in Christ '; otherwise they were not. In
one of his last extant writings, Phil. iii. 4, Paul
says : ' If anyone else thinks he has confidence
after the flesh, I have it more ; circumcised on
the eighth day, of the race of Israel, of the tribe
of Benjamin, a Hebrew of the Hebrews, a Pharisee
in accordance with the Law, persecuting the Church
in zeal, having become irreproachable in accordance with righteousness in the Law. But all these
things which were gain to me, I have reckoned
loss because of Christ. In fact I reckon all things
loss because of the surpassing character of the
knowledge of Jesus Christ my Lord, for whose
sake I lost all things, and I reckon them as baubles
in order that I may gain Christ and be found in
him, not having my righteousness derived from
the Law but the righteousness which comes through
faith in Christ, the righteousness derived from God
on the basis of faith.'

This statement introduces other ideas which we
shall have to consider later (p. 213). For the moment, the point to seize is Paul's extreme pride
in his race and in its Law. He had not been a
Gentile, no : nor had he been a careless, negligent
Jew : he had been an enthusiast for a correctness
which appeared the most important thing in life,
and which even in distant retrospect seemed no

small achievement. His constant emphasis in the earlier letters that he had no boast save in Christ indicates that this sort of pride was for him a realized danger. As he says in Gal. i. 14, ' I was making progress in the Jewish way of living— (*ioudaismos* means that, as we can see from the corresponding *hellenismos*)—beyond many contemporaries in my race, being in a more exceeding degree an enthusiast for the ancestral traditions which I inherited ' (it is not simply ' ancestral traditions ' ; there is a genitive of the personal pronoun to point the sense).

In Romans there is no doubt that the Jew is God's first choice among mankind, and in spite of Jewish resistance to Christian teaching and Jewish unwillingness to become ' in Christ ', Paul persists in the believing hope that all Israel is ultimately to fulfil its glorious destiny in Christ (xi.). He rejects the Law, but in so doing he appeals to an earlier springtime, the Call of Abraham, the father of all Jews and, for Paul, of all who now follow the way of faith.

Modern students of Judaism have drawn attention to Paul's misrepresentation of Pharisaism— and in particular to his statement [1] that any man under the Law who failed to keep the whole Law was accursed. Although it was said that the breach of one commandment was the breach of all and the keeping of one was the keeping of all, this

[1] A parallel in James ii. 10.

statement is certainly misleading. The observance of the Law did not for a Jew involve the pitiless antithesis of complete success and complete failure which Paul here portrays, since in Jewish belief no idea was more stressed than the infinite and unceasing willingness of God to forgive the penitent sinner. To an orthodox Jew the Christian controversies on the possibility of forgiveness of post-baptismal sin would have appeared a blasphemous limitation of divine power. Certain categories of men were excluded from a share in the life of the World to Come : that was God's free will ; but for Israel, at least, chastening and forgiveness would be the order of the day until the consummation of all things.

Nevertheless, we can understand why Paul spoke as he did. First, he was a Pharisee ; he was not, and never claims to have been, a Scribe. That is to say, his sympathies were with the extreme orthodox party : but, familiar as he clearly was with the interpretation of the Law, he did not claim to be an expert. Between a Scribe and a Pharisee there could be as much difference as between one of the early English Tractarians who with Newman and Pusey translated early Christian writers and reprinted seventeenth-century Anglican divines in the ' Library of Anglo-Catholic Theology ' on the one hand, and a lay subscriber to the *Church Times* on the other. A Pharisee could be more rigorous than a Scribe : and he had Deut. xxvii. 26

and xxviii. 58–9 to inspire the idea. If the custom described somewhat later in the Jewish law-book called the Mishna existed then, Paul heard the latter text recited as a refrain during each of his scourgings in the synagogue. Secondly, he is speaking as a convert and as a convert whose conversion had involved a radical *volte-face*. Earlier convictions, passionately held and then passionately abandoned after a volcanic internal crisis, cannot but present themselves in distorted shapes. Thirdly, Paul's major writings are all writings of controversy. He was fighting on several fronts : and his weapon was the *reductio ad absurdum*. In any case, Rabbinic training has left its mark on him—not least in his habit of arguing from isolated texts in what has been called a fragmentary style, in the forms in which he introduces scriptural quotations, and in his way of combining such quotations with a running commentary.

Acts xxii. 3 makes him describe himself at Jerusalem as having been reared in that city and thoroughly trained at the feet of Gamaliel.[1] In the same book we read (vii. 58) that the men who stoned Stephen for his provocative utterances about the Temple laid their garments by the feet of a young man called Saul (viii. 3), that Saul savagely harassed the Church, entering into houses and carrying off men and women, putting them in prison, and (ix. 1) that Saul went to the high

[1] A distinguished teacher of the liberal school of Hillel.

priest and requested of him letters to the synagogues of Damascus, so that he might bring in bonds to Jerusalem any whom he found on the way, men and women alike : then on the road to Damascus happened the event which we shall consider in the next chapter.

This account raises a serious difficulty. Paul's persecution of Christians is an established fact, for he makes repeated references to it, as for instance 1 Cor. xv. 9 : ' For I am the least of the Apostles, who am not worthy to be called an Apostle, because I persecuted the Church of Christ,' and Gal. i. 13 : ' Beyond measure I persecuted the church of God and ravaged it.' Nevertheless, in this same passage of Galatians, marked as it is by great solemnity (i. 20, ' What I write to you, lo, in God's sight I tell no lie ') and in answer to enemies who would be quick to seize on any error of fact, he says of the time after his conversion (i. 22) : ' And I was not known by sight to the churches in Christ of Judaea : but they knew only by what they heard, that he who once persecuted us now preaches the faith which he once savagely attacked, and they glorified God in me.'[1] Critics have therefore urged that the narrative of Acts is to be rejected entirely, and that Paul's activity as a persecutor must be assigned to his own home in Tarsus. This con-

[1] Also Gal. i. 17, after the conversion, ' I did not *go up* to Jerusalem '—not, as we might expect if we accept the testimony of Acts, ' I did not *return* to Jerusalem '

tention cannot be dismissed out of hand, and Paul's presence at the death of Stephen, like Gamaliel's advocacy of a ' wait and see ' policy before the Sanhedrin or Jewish Council at Jerusalem, do look a little like literary devices intended to prepare the reader for his intense activity in chapters xiii. to xxviii. Nevertheless, Paul's adversaries later spoke of his physical presence as weak (2 Cor. x. 10) and, if we assume that he had a hand in the persecution of Christians at Jerusalem but was not as prominent in it as was thought later, he may not have been noticed. Further, although Christianity spread fast from the beginning through the synagogues of the Dispersion, can we suppose that there was already room for activity by a persecutor at Tarsus ? Paul says ' unknown by sight to the churches ', the communities as such did not know him by sight ; but his name was known as a persecutor, and the hatred felt against him in the Christian community of Jerusalem is most naturally understood if his activities had lain there. His presence at Stephen's death may be doubted, and his mission to Damascus was probably what may be called official propaganda : a mission for the Sanhedrin to stir up the local Jews to apply the discipline of the synagogue to men now regarded as apostates.

Probably Paul had been at Jerusalem, as man if not as boy ; all his words are meant to prove is his independence of Palestinian Christianity.

33

In any case, we know that he had been a zealous Jew, had persecuted Christians, and, as a result of what he held to be a direct revelation, ceased to persecute them and became a supremely energetic teacher and organizer of the new movement. We must now consider the implications both of his persecution and of this conversion.

CHAPTER III

DAMASCUS

WHEN Paul first learned of the body which was the germ cell of later Christianity, there was no title ' Christian ' : that came into being at Antioch, and perhaps as a nickname. The fact which Paul encountered was the existence of a body of Jews and proselytes who held a peculiar view of the ' hope of Israel ' (p. 25, above). This ' hope ' was widespread and held not only by Pharisees who were versed in the Law, but also by Galilaeans, who were not. Accordingly, it assumed various forms : its denial would have been unpopular in some circles (not indeed among the Sadducees who controlled the Temple), but neither its denial nor the choice or creation of a particular form of it would at this time have involved unorthodoxy. The norm of Judaism was belief in the Oneness of God and observance of the Law ; its battle-cries were the Law, the People, and the Temple. Unless these were attacked, complete unquestioning tolerance prevailed. Even the Essenes, who eschewed the worship of the Temple, were unassailed. The Pharisees might wish all men to be even as they

35

were ; but that result could be attained only by persuasion.

The ' hope of Israel ' involved not the destruction but the fulfilment of the Law. As with Jerusalem and the Temple, so with the Law the end (as usually conceived) would be not destruction but glorification : just as the new Jerusalem would descend from heaven without spot or blemish, so would the Law be perfectly observed and the people abide in a new purity as God's people. ' Thy Kingdom come ' has the same meaning as ' Thy will be done on earth as it is in heaven ', and a pious Jew would have no difficulty in uttering either petition.[1] In the Kingdom many prescripts would be unnecessary : but the Law would constitute the norm of the judgment and its study would remain as an occupation thereafter.

The approaching end of the present world order, in which the heathen triumphed and the chosen people were afflicted, would be heralded by certain signs. On the one hand, God would send certain forerunners—a returning Moses and Elijah. On the other, the forces of evil would, as it were, be intensified and would push their ascendancy to the length of a second profanation of the Holy Place

---

[1] Though he would have preferred ' till thy Kingdom be manifested, manifest itself, or appear '. Whenever men obeyed the Law, they took ' the yoke of the Kingdom ' upon themselves. Cf. Wisdom x. 10, ' (Wisdom) showed to him the sovereignty of God.'

at Jerusalem, comparable with that for which Anti-ochus Epiphanes had been responsible. Then, at what seemed the darkest hour, God's Anointed would appear to captain God's people, and to lead them in that last desperate struggle which must end in victory.

In the first century of our era, probably in the third decade, a Jewish ascetic now known as John the Baptist assumed the long-disused rôle of prophet and called his fellow-countrymen to repentance in the preparation for the coming of the Kingdom in the near future. Such repentance had long been regarded as a necessary preliminary. John's hearers were to change the direction of their lives, and as seal and symbol of this they were to plunge into the River Jordan ; that would be a guarantee of efficacious repentance and of safety in the impending judgment. John's message found a wide acceptance in a time of troubled hearts and minds, and, while it might seem politically dangerous, it was theologi-cally unexceptionable. Christian posterity thought of this as the divinely appointed prelude to Jesus of Nazareth, whose teaching activity began after John was thrown into prison.

The work of Jesus was the direct, forceful and authoritative summoning of men to the life of the Kingdom. That Kingdom was not yet come visibly, yet by anticipation it existed already in him and among those who would follow him. Very soon it would come with power ; meanwhile those whom God had chosen to a share in it must make their calling and election sure, and to this end must sacrifice all personal interests and attachments, blameless and even praiseworthy as they would have been in normal times. There was naturally a certain fluctuation between ' being chosen ' and ' choosing '. God chose whom he would ; they could refuse this privilege, and others might then take their place in the Kingdom, yet without being sure till the end that they would enjoy it. This is expressed in the parable of the wedding feast as told in Matt. xxii. : some refuse to answer the call and their places are filled by others ; one answers a call and arrives, but is rejected as not having a wedding garment. Further, predestination (which is here conceived as the personal choice of a personal God, and not as the impersonal ordinance of fate such as Greek astrology taught) did not exclude or diminish man's moral responsibility of choice.

Jesus claimed in some sort a Messianic position, although the question of the terminology which he used is extremely difficult, and perhaps insoluble. In any case, he clearly revived the prophetic conception of Judaism and claimed the right to interpret the Law without reference to tradition, and even to dispense men from Sabbath observances, on his own authority fortified by reasoning from first principles : further, he held the preaching of the message and the following of it to be more urgent than normal obligations (Matt. viii. 21 ; Luke ix.

59), and he rejected any scruples about ritual impurity which debarred from religious influences the men who most needed them. The claim to interpret the Law was natural if Jesus was Messiah, for it was believed that the Messiah, when he came, would interpret the Law, and the Law so interpreted was occasionally called ' the Torah of the Messiah '.[1] This was provocative, both to Pharisaic orthodoxy which valued tradition as supplementing and interpreting the written law, and also to Sadducee conservatism which clung to the letter of the law. At the same time, certain prophecies of Jesus, which appeared to imply an impending destruction of the Temple, were offensive in the last degree to popular sentiment in general.

Opposition grew, and it became clear to Jesus that an attempt would be made to put him to death. He in his turn probably had no difficulty in believing that this death might be willed by God as part of the necessary preliminaries for the establishment of the Kingdom ' with power '. We read in Mark x. 45 : ' For indeed the Son of man came not to be served but to serve and to give his life as a ransom for (*or* in place of) many.' That may be (as Schweitzer suggests) the Son of man is to die, and his death will by God be permitted to take the place of the general sufferings of the elect which

[1] Matt. xi. 29 (peculiar to Matthew), ' Take my yoke upon you ' implies a special ' yoke ' in contrast to that of the Law as understood.

were commonly expected to precede the Messianic
rule.   In any case, to ' ransom ' Israel was a regular
function of the Messiah as generally conceived.   It
was a new ' ransoming ' parallel to the delivery from
Egypt and the still earlier ' ransoming ' by circumcision.   For a moment the disciples would be
scattered, but only Jesus would die ; and he may
well have expected that his death would at once
be followed by his appearance in clouds of glory,
by the overthrow of the forces of evil, and by the
judgment of the world.   A new order was beginning,
a new covenant of God for his elect : and like the
covenant in Exod. xxiv. 8, and that of the circumcision, it must be sealed in blood.   Hence the
prophetic act and words of symbolism at the Last
Supper (Mark xiv. 22–4), ' This is my body,' ' This
is my blood of the covenant poured out for many.' [1]

[1] The word translated ' covenant ' is *diatheke*.   In
secular Greek this is usually ' will ', ' testament ', but
can mean ' compact ' (in particular a compact in which
one of the parties is put under obligation not to do
certain things) ; the cognate verb covers ' compact ',
' agreement ', and ' ordinance '.   The ' covenants ' of
God and Israel subsequent to that of Sinai are ordi-
nances providing mercy if Israel would keep certain
conditions.   The word in the Septuagint describes those
divine undertakings to God's human partner, Israel,
which constituted the nature of their relationship.   (The
translation ' dispensation ' is preferred by many ; there
is little difference of meaning, except that ' covenant '
has, perhaps, the merit of emphasizing the intimacy of
Israel with God.   Nevertheless, Israel could not of course

The simple solemnity with which Jews shared bread and cup was made the acted parable both to explain the imminent event and to associate the disciples with it. ' Verily, verily I say unto you that I will drink no more of the fruit of the vine till that day when I drink it new in the kingdom of God.'

The price was paid, but the heavens did not open : to the Jewish authorities, and for the moment to the disciples, this must have seemed to be the end of the story. The disciples had hoped (Luke xxiv. 21) ' that he it is who should ransom Israel '. And now in the hour of despair their hope was brought to a new and different life by appearances of Jesus as the risen Messiah (1 Cor. xv. 4), ' he was seen of Cephas, then of the Twelve ; then he was seen of above 500 brethren at one time, of whom the greater part survive till now, though some are fallen on sleep ; then he was seen of James, and thereafter of all the Apostles '.[1] The forces of evil—and they were not conceived as abstractions — had not triumphed. The Book of Acts describes the disciples as waiting, for a time, passively for God's next and final intervention in the world's history, and then on the day of Pentecost undergoing a

make terms with God.) The other sense of *diatheke*, ' will ', is sometimes implicit in Pauline usage, where it is linked to the traditional metaphors of inheritance, adoption, and sonship—which describe the relationship in another way.

[1] On the meaning of this word, see p. 50, later.

collective experience of the descent of the Spirit upon them in their assembly. This is the birthday of the Church, as the appearance to ' above 500 brethren ' was in the other tradition.

Whatever we suppose to have happened then, the Spirit was held to be a primary characteristic of the Christian body. The life of men obviously depends on the power to breathe : and according to Gen. ii. 7 when God made man he ' breathed into his nostrils the breath of life ; and man became a living soul '. The Jews were familiar also with writings and traditions of men called prophets, who spoke not as of themselves but as of God. It was natural to interpret these utterances, and also exceptional gifts of courage, skill and the like, as due to a special kind of breath, *pneuma*, which came upon them from God—what we mean by inspiration. This spirit of God is something conferred on them for a purpose, as it was believed to have been conferred upon all the writers of the books of the Old Testament : these writers had, so to speak, acted as God's amanuenses. In the time of Jesus prophecy was commonly regarded as a divine gift which had been withdrawn for centuries from the Jewish people. There would be no more prophecy till the ' days of the Messiah ' or till just before them.[1] Then there would be a gift of this Spirit to the Messiah

---

[1] But certain Rabbis had the ' spirit ' or were deemed worthy of it. In the Old Testament the Spirit can be the source of morality (Ps. li. 12).

and to the people of Israel in general : it would be one of the miracles characteristic of the period and would produce the resurrection of the dead (Ezek. xxxvii. 14). In the words of Joel ii. 28, which are put in Peter's mouth at Pentecost in Acts ii. 17, ' And it shall come to pass afterward that I will pour out my spirit upon all flesh ; and your sons and your daughters shall prophesy, your old men shall dream dreams, your young men shall see visions ; and also upon the servants and upon the handmaids in those days will I pour out my spirit.'

In Acts this corporate experience is made to lead directly to the first preaching activity of Peter, who was clearly the strongest personality in the community. Hesitation and inactivity were ended. God would bring the visible Kingdom when he wished : meanwhile, the Resurrection appearances had authorized those who had known and followed Jesus to continue his work of teaching and to do their best to enable Israel to realize its divine destiny. They were therefore compelled to shape a message of their own. Jesus in his lifetime had sent out disciples to herald the coming of the Kingdom, but their duty had been clear and simple ; they had only to give a note of urgency to ideas which were widely disseminated, and behind them was a visible and active Jesus engaged in the work of teaching and healing. Now Jesus had died the death of a common criminal at the hands of those aliens whom a Messianic king would have been expected to chase from the city which their presence profaned. So far as we know, no Jew had ever previously envisaged the Messiah as dying.

Yet the disciples, unless they decided that they had been the victims of an illusion, could not but believe that, since the death had happened, it must have been divinely intended. Further, if it was divinely intended, it must also have been contained in Old Testament prophecy, since one of the chief marks of Messiahship was the fulfilment of prophecy. Accordingly the Scriptures were searched, and certain prophecies in the Old Testament were so interpreted. Particular importance attaches to Isa. liii., the description of the Servant of the Lord despised and rejected of men, by whose stripes we were healed, who shall justify many (that is, give them the standing of being just),[1] bearing their sins —a prophecy which as written probably referred to the people of Israel ; and to Hos. vi. 2, ' After two days he will revive us : in the third day he will raise us up, and we shall live in his sight '—which gave the ' third day ' on which Jesus was believed to have been raised from the dead ; and to certain passages in the Psalms. We may think all this artificial, because for us the exegesis of a scriptural book, as of any other, is the attempt to discover what a particular author living in a particular time and place

[1] This last phrase does not appear in the New Testament citations of prophecy.

meant to say. A Jew faced with a passage in holy writ had an altogether different attitude of mind ; inspired writing contained all truth. If you did not elicit this by a straightforward interpretation, you might and must properly apply all your subtlety to elicit it otherwise. You could not apprehend anything true which was novel and which was not somehow included in revelation.[1] Many Greeks read Homer and later Plato in a similar spirit.

Christian theology begins not with Paul's thinking but with this self-adjustment of the church at Jerusalem to the death of Jesus and with its correlation of that death to the Old Testament. The searching of the Scriptures and the beginning of those collections and combinations of proof texts which were used for centuries afterwards was not a mere apologetic device but was a central aspect of the community's self-justification. Furthermore, we must assign to this earliest period of Christian life the beginnings of Christology.

The Messiah in Jewish thought was a divine functionary greater than any of the sons of men, sometimes thought to be pre-existent in the sense that God had made him like other beings and had him ready for use : but the Messiah existed only in reference to his Messianic functions, and he would simply appear in order to perform them. Now, so far as we can see, the use of Messianic titulature by Jesus was very restricted and did not

[1] Cf. Romans xv. 4.

form part of his first approach to disciples or of his approach to the world in general ; furthermore, the concept of Messiahship was far from being precise and definite.

Jesus in his first and every approach to men claimed not only a divine mission, but also a peculiar authority and created the sense of authority, ' not as the scribes '. The impression which he made was immeasurably deepened, as well as interpreted, by the conviction that he was Messiah and by the transference to him of attributes from various conceptions which were related to that expected figure. So the theology was elaborated : but the point of departure for its makers was an immediate, instinctive response to what seemed innate leadership. Jesus as Messiah was a person and not merely a functionary ; and he seemed, as a person, to fall outside the ordinary categories. The story of the Transfiguration (Mark ix. ; Matt. xvii. ; Luke ix.) represents an experience of the three chosen disciples and an attitude formed during the life of Jesus without which the Resurrection stories would hardly be intelligible.[1] The pause which now manifestly existed between the death and resurrection on the one hand and the completion of Messianic work on the other involved a continuous active life of Jesus as a supernatural being, *Maran* (' Our Lord ') ; no mere personified effluence of God, but an active

[1] That Jesus said anything like Matt. xi. 27 (= Luke x. 22) is very doubtful, but he could be credited with it.

personality, and though subordinate to God, yet superior to all other beings, visible and invisible. He was Servant of God, and Son of God, a phrase which did not involve physical relationship, but described a position (Rom. i. 4). All later glorification of the place and power of Jesus could follow from this.

Nevertheless, in the teaching of this early period, the emphasis was no doubt in the main on the smallness of the change to be made in a traditional Jewish piety. The speeches in the early part of the Acts may preserve something of the spirit of those days. They represent the death of Jesus not as a necessary atonement for sin, but as an unfortunate incident, a forgivable error on the part of the rulers and people of the Jews. There was still time for repentance and for entering into the blessings which Jesus could bestow on his return in glory. In spite of this, the absence of the idea of atonement from the preaching as recorded may be due to a modification of primitive sources. Decisive evidence is afforded by 1 Cor. xv. 3. Paul, in his summary of the doctrine which he himself received and later delivered to the Corinthians, includes ' that Christ died for our sins according to the Scriptures ' ; ' for us all ' is axiomatic also in Rom. viii. 32. The Death was a necessity ; in this way Christ brought the redemption expected of the Messiah ; Isa. liii. had pointed to the idea of vicarious suffering.[1]

[1] Cf. p. 199, later.

The theology of this period is rudimentary, but it deserves the name of theology. Emphatically as Paul claimed to teach a Gospel revealed to him by the Lord and not by men, his version of the Christian *kerygma*, ' proclamation ', agrees closely with that represented in the earlier chapters of Acts, and with the agreed summary which Paul himself quotes at the beginning of Romans. The fulfilment of prophecy, the saving events of the life of Jesus, the outpouring of the spirit : these were the visible pledges of the presence of the new age. It was marked also by an increased directness of approach to God as ' Abba, Father ' (Rom viii. 15). Wherever Paul was founding a community, his teaching started with these things : he added further and more complex instruction in proportion to the capacity which his hearers and readers showed, or in answer to their needs (1 Cor. ii. 6).

We see thus the beginnings of Christian theology. These earliest days include also the beginnings of church order and organization. The community as it met was no casual aggregation of like-minded men : it was the divinely chosen *ekklesia tou theou*, the solemn assembly of the people of God, a concept which recalled Deut. xxiii. 2 and the whole history of Israel's election. The members of this community were *hagioi*, ' holy ', ' consecrated ' like the ' saints of the Most High ', whose kingdom was, in Dan. vii. 9–28, the manifestation of the Son of man. When other communities came into being, this title

applied primarily to the members of the mother
church of Jerusalem. The term *ekklesia* came to
be applied to the local groups of Christians in
various places, meeting, acting, or considered as a
whole and was used in the plural, which Paul likes,
but there was no distinct word for ' community ' or
' congregation '.

The *ekklesia* had its leaders. Jesus had called
twelve followers to whom he had given a rank which
raised them above the other disciples. At the consummation of all things, they were to sit on twelve
thrones judging the twelve tribes of Israel. What
they bound on earth was to be bound in heaven ;
what they loosed on earth was to be loosed in
heaven. If this is not a saying of Jesus, at least it
expresses an early consciousness of authority and
is the Rabbinic way of saying that their decisions
on questions of conduct were to be authoritative.
The Twelve had their predestined functions in the
Kingdom, when it should come with power. Meanwhile, they had this anticipatory authority and
prestige. By the side of the Twelve James the
brother of Jesus took his place. He had not been
a disciple of the living Jesus, but an appearance of
the risen Lord won him to the movement, in which
he thereafter enjoyed the standing due to his relationship. James, Peter and John had special authority
within the group (p. 110, later).

This central body has a peculiar dignity. An
important position seems to belong also to the group

of Apostles ' to whom Christ appeared ' according to
I Cor. xv. 7. The term means simply ' delegates ',
' men commissioned to the service of the Gospel ',
and here implies a direct commission from God and
a call to preach. In this passage the term probably
refers to the Twelve. Paul's claim to the title, and
the way in which his adversaries questioned that
claim (pp. 161, 200, later); imply the narrower sense
of an appointment by Christ, verified by the ability
to work miracles (2 Cor. xii. 12); but he uses it
also in a broader sense, which survived for a time,
to mean any emissaries chosen by a community,
whether that of Jerusalem or another (2 Cor. viii.
23; Phil. ii. 25). Administrative offices were gradually created to serve practical needs. *Diakonoi*
seemed to have been responsible for the Greek-
speaking part of the Jerusalem community and for
some missionary activity, and in Phil. i. 1 we find
them mentioned after *episkopoi*, ' overseers ', a term
destined for a great history as ' bishops '. We hear
also of a body of *presbyteroi*, ' elders ', who seem
to be the governing body of the church of Jerusalem
and perhaps came into being when the Christian
movement was spreading; if the Twelve were
concerned with the Church as a whole, there was
need of a local government patterned on that of the
Jewish groups of the Dispersion.

Presbyteroi, diakonoi [1] and *episkopoi* are administrative officers chosen by communities; on the

[1] In Rom. xvi. 1 we find a woman with this title.

other hand the Twelve or Apostles in the narrower sense, the *prophetai* (men who were suddenly seized by the Spirit and uttered inspired messages), and the *didaskaloi*, or teachers, were regarded as chosen by the Lord. Of course, the antithesis is not absolute, and in 1 Cor. xii. 28 helpers and administrators are classed together with apostles, prophets, teachers, miracle-workers, and men with the gift of tongues, and all are regarded as divinely appointed. This is natural, since the action of the community could be seen as the action of God. Nevertheless, there is a distinction between officials as of God and officials as of the community whom the community could make and unmake. The hierarchy of later Christendom was here in germ. We shall see later that Paul adopted an attitude which was somewhat different from that of Jerusalem (p. 103, later) ; but for Paul also teacher and taught are in a steady antithesis, even though it is an antithesis coloured by humility. Paul claimed full authority to regulate the lives of the churches which he founded, and expected these churches to obey the men who took the lead in them, and furthermore he regarded a community as capable of passing in agreement with him a sentence of excommunication which would be ratified in Heaven (cf. p. 177, later) : in writing to the church of Rome, which he had not founded, he makes no such claims.

The co-existence of these two types of office corresponded to a certain duality in the community's life : on the one hand, straightforward normal activity, on the other, manifestations of the Spirit, which is in the main in Acts i–xii. a divine intrusive force which cannot be denied and which it would be blasphemous to resist (the Spirit is not here, as in Paul, a steady control and a regular and normative principle of religious life).

No one in the original group of disciples at Jerusalem had any notion that his loyalty to Jesus involved or could involve any breach with the national religion of Israel. Just as Israel had always been a small band living among the great peoples of the earth, but not ashamed of its smallness, so within the small band there was at many times a smaller band.

> The faithful few fought bravely
> To guard the nation's life.

Tradition told of the 7,000 who had not bowed the knee to Baal : the whole line of prophets and many of the writers of the Psalms had the feelings of members of a self-conscious minority. The Pharisees had started as a small group of enthusiasts united by a desire for the more accurate observation of the Law. On each occasion the minority in question held itself to be the true representative of Israel's heritage and mission, and sought to appeal to the conscience of other Jews, to awaken them, and to bring them into line.

The men who believed themselves to have seen

the Risen Lord and to have received a commission from him thought likewise. Consequently, there was no idea of staying away from the Temple and no immediate slackening in loyalty to the Law. The Passover was observed, though its association in time with the death of Jesus introduced new thoughts of sorrow for the nation's failure to accept him. The continuity of Christianity with Judaism is most strikingly illustrated by the preservation of Passover observance in Gentile Christian communities. Whether or not it was observed from the beginning in churches which were predominantly so composed, it soon was and developed into the Christian Easter, and in 1 Cor. v. 7 Paul can speak of the Passover (whether observance or tradition) as a matter which will be familiar.[1]

---

[1] This observance could only at Jerusalem be the full Passover including the eating of the Paschal lamb by groups of ten to twenty persons, for that ceremony depended on the existence of the Temple in which the sacrifice could be made ; when the Temple disappeared, so did the full rite. But, even earlier, millions of Jews could be at Jerusalem for the feast at most but once in their lives : they had to content themselves with observing in their own homes the abstinence from leaven, the drinking of the prescribed cups, the eating of the bitter herbs, and the solemn commemoration of God's deliverance of Israel out of Egypt. Such a ceremony had its obvious fitness even for Christians who were not of Jewish extraction. Through the death of Jesus they had gained entry to their promised land, and the deliverance of Israel from Egypt was a regular type of the new salvation

At the same time, the Christians of Jerusalem constituted a group. There was nothing heterodox or separatist in this : ' Every assembly which is for the sake of Heaven will in the end be established ; and one that is not for the sake of Heaven will in the end not be established.'[1] Any ten male Jews could form a synagogue and share the reading of Scripture, the word of exhortation, and the expression of prayer and praise. The disciples of Jesus had lived in intimate fellowship with him. They had eaten and drunk with him and they continued to eat and drink together after his death. A Jew did not eat or drink without blessing God's name, and the blessing had particular solemnity when the meal was a social meal. Special thanksgivings were attached to the bread broken by the host at the beginning of the meal and to the ' Cup of blessing ' drunk at its close.

This is the beginning of Christian Eucharistic worship, the very name *eucharistia*, ' thanksgiving ', customary from the end of the first century, the opening of the central prayer in so many liturgies with ' We thank Thee, God . . .', and the fact that the reference to the Last Supper is always made (cf. p. 184, later). The full celebration of the Passover was not only limited to Jerusalem, but also restricted most rigorously to circumcised persons, and popular feeling on this point, which was explicitly ordered in Exodus, was very strong.

[1] Pirkē Aboth (R. H. Charles, *Apocrypha and Pseudepigrapha of the Old Testament*, 2, p. 705), iv. 14.

in a parenthetic form, indicate the ultimate deriva-
tion of the ceremony from a Jewish benediction of
shared food : so does the Pauline phrase (1 Cor. x.
16) ' the cup of blessing ', where the word for blessing, *eulogia*, is that which appears on a Jewish cup.

We can form some idea of the general type of this
early worship from material, probably not later than
A.D. 100, in a document known as the *Teaching
of the Twelve Apostles*. This contains a model form of
Eucharistic prayer which is no more than an elaboration of this Jewish custom and of the traditional
Jewish prayer that God would lift a basket to gather
the scattered members of the nation of Israel from
the four ends of the earth into their own land :
custom and prayer are adapted to the disciples'
loving memory of their past fellowship with Jesus
and to their hopeful anticipation of his promised
return. The cup [1] is blessed with the words :

We give Thee thanks, Our Father, for the holy vine
of David Thy servant, which Thou hast made known

---

[1] The cup comes first here, as in the shorter text of
Luke xxii. 15 ff. This corresponds to the blessing of
cup and bread which introduced the Sabbath : there
too we find the phrase ' Cup of blessing ' and this cup
(unlike that after a meal) was regularly passed round.
(The cup which Jesus blessed may have been a goblet,
the contents of which were distributed in individual cups.)
This priority of Cup may be explained on the hypothesis
that, when the usage became weekly and not daily, some
circles of Jewish Christians assimilated it to the rite
which introduced the Sabbath.

to us through Thy servant[1] Jesus : glory be to Thee for ever.

The broken bread is blessed thus :

We give Thee thanks, Our Father, for the life and knowledge which Thou hast made known to us through Jesus Thy servant : glory be to Thee for ever. As this bread was scattered on the mountains and, when gathered, became one, so let Thy Church be gathered together from the ends of the world into Thy Kingdom : for Thine is the glory and power through Jesus Christ for ever.

After all have partaken, this solemn thanksgiving follows :

We give Thee thanks, holy Father, for Thy holy Name, which Thou didst make to tabernacle in our hearts, and for the knowledge and faith and immortality which Thou didst make known to us through Jesus Thy servant : glory be to Thee for ever. Thou, almighty Ruler, didst create all things for Thy Name's sake. Food and drink hast Thou given to men for their enjoyment, that they may offer thanks to Thee : but to us Thou hast given spiritual food and drink and eternal life through Thy servant. Above all we give thanks to Thee for Thy power : glory be to Thee for ever. Remember, O Lord, Thy Church, to rescue it from all evil and to perfect it in Thy love, and bring it together from the four winds, a Church sanctified, into Thy Kingdom, which Thou hast prepared for it, for Thine is the power and the glory for ever.

Let grace come, and let this world pass away.
Hosanna to the God of David.

---

[1] The word throughout translated ' servant ' can also mean ' son '.

If anyone is holy, let him come : if anyone is not, let him repent. *Marana tha* (' Come, Lord '). Amen.

These prayers represent the result of development and elaboration, but they seem to reproduce the genius of the Eucharist of the early days.

The common meal of the Christians is frequently described as the ' breaking of bread ', and various testimonies indicate that on occasions there was bread and salt (an inevitable concomitant in a Jewish meal), and no liquid but water. This may be due to the ascetic tendencies of James the Just, who drank no wine, and of other like-minded men, some of whom may have been former followers of John the Baptist ; Paul's desire in Rom. xiv. 21 that the scruples of total abstainers should be considered may imply that he would have tolerated a wineless Eucharist. Nevertheless, the accusation that Jesus was a wine-bibber suggests that ascetic tendencies did not dominate Christian beginnings, and wine was an essential part of a Jewish social meal and of the blessing which ushered in the Sabbath.[1] It is more reasonable to assume that the wine was an original element sometimes omitted than that it was a later addition.[2]

[1] In modern times the blessing which should be spoken over wine is sometimes spoken over bread when there is no wine.

[2] Note that in the *Teaching of the Twelve Apostles*, xiv. 1, ' break bread ' is used to refer to the rite, although, as we have seen, it included a blessing of a cup.

At first, it seems, after the Resurrection the disciples met every day, perhaps in daily expectation that Jesus would manifest himself in final glory at the time of their breaking of bread. When they acquired that new consciousness of purpose which Acts associates with Pentecost, and were launched on their new life of active work, the expectation was no less vivid, no less the dominant element in their corporate and individual existences. Nevertheless, the meal came to be weekly and not daily and was associated with the Lord's Day (a title which appears first in Rev. i. 10, but is probably older), the day after the Sabbath, on which Jesus was believed to have manifested himself as a risen being, and itself acquired the title in Greek of *kyriakon deipnon*, the Lord's Supper. It was an evening meal; in the ancient world men took a little food at other times, but there was only one ' meal ' *par excellence* in the day,[1] and that was in the late afternoon or early evening, when the ordinary occupations of the day were over.

The Sabbath was still observed and continued to be observed by Jewish communities, but this selection of a new holy day, like Mohammed's choice of Friday, shows a consciousness of novelty which characterized the movement in spite of its fidelity to Jewish tradition. It was the true Israel

[1] Apart from the Jewish Sabbath, which had three stated meals, and the exceptional midday meal of the Essenes.

of God and it marked its difference. This appears also in the choice of Wednesday and Friday, in preference to Monday and Thursday, as days of fasting.[1] The choice of Friday involved, in fact, a breach of a Jewish custom (cf. Jud. viii. 6), but this custom did not belong to the Law in the strict sense and was not universally observed. Not merely Sunday, but the Jewish week was adopted by all Christian communities. These things should always be remembered, since, like the Jewish hours of daily prayer and the Jewish grace at meals, they involved an extraordinary change of habit for Gentile converts. The planetary week was at this very time spreading through the world, although its acceptance was slow. At the same time, no one who was not a Jew had lived with his life thus punctuated by a weekly religious observance : paganism had its periods of special devotion, as, for instance, to Isis or Cybele, but nothing like this steady thread running through the continuity of daily life. These institutions contributed greatly to the creation of a way of life which, while it might not tell with full force on the first generation of converts, was bound to make a background of otherness for their children.

The Christian movement began against the background of the teaching and activity of John the Baptist. John, as we saw, made baptism the rite

[1] We may doubt whether Paul's converts in general adopted any such custom.

necessary for safety in the Judgment which was to come. Jesus himself received this baptism ; and, when his disciples set about their task of seeking to prepare Israel for the impending Day of the Lord, they naturally applied the ceremony to all who wished to join their number. In the earliest phase there can have been no preliminary training as a condition of admission.[1] The disciples, like John, would associate with the rite the belief that those baptized, and thus admitted to the Kingdom, obtained remission of past sins and were sealed as members of the Kingdom. In some way which cannot be clearly defined, they associated with it also the belief that those baptized would receive the gift of the Spirit—the new powers which were now bestowed by God upon those who already, by anticipation, shared in the Messianic Kingdom.

This life was marked by the pious practice of fasting (p. 59) which had been characteristic of the disciples of John the Baptist, and by a great intensity of fellowship and brotherly love and mutual benefaction, which is said to have gone to the length of a sharing of property : certainly there was much charity within the group and the way in which Paul's

[1] Some of Paul's difficulties at Corinth arose from this. Parables such as Matt. xiii. 47 ff., xxii. 1 ff., imply that the net is to be cast as widely as possible ; the winnowing comes at the day of Judgment. The work was to be done against time, unlike the admission of proselytes to Judaism, which was preceded by catechetical instruction such as Christianity later employed.

Gentile converts later had to support the Mother Church could be the result of a period of intense goodwill secured by living on capital. But the closeness of the fellowship did not in itself entail any risk of persecution or even pressure from the Jewish authorities or other Jews. While Jesus lived, the movement involved a possible menace to public order : after his death the continued cohesion of his disciples, and their conviction that, in spite of the Crucifixion, Jesus was the Messiah and would come again in glory as God's minister of judgment, would at first appear harmless folly. The Sanhedrin may, as Acts iv. and v. says, have called representative disciples for a hearing : we cannot know.

Nevertheless, this appearance of tranquillity was deceptive. A religious movement can develop very fast in its early days : in this movement belief in the Spirit could legitimize breaches with tradition. Jesus had not been concerned with any preaching to Gentiles : his mission was to his own people ; some Gentiles would be in the Kingdom, but they would be those whom God had chosen. Yet the attitude of Jesus towards the Law had involved an independence which was bitterly resented, and the whole attitude of the disciples implied that the official representatives of Judaism had been false guides. The men from Galilee had themselves lived in a world in which there was much of Gentile life and Gentile ways : the early group at Jerusalem included not only them but also Jews who had spent time in the Dispersion and returned to Jerusalem, and such men (like Paul) were liable not only to fanaticism but also to a certain independence ; even their orthodoxy would often have a somewhat different ethos from that of the natives of Jerusalem, and they would readily be suspected of innovation. The appointment of the *diakonoi* (p. 50) resulted from the pressure of such men within the Christian community, and it is of great importance that one of the Seven was a proselyte. Just as Peter stood out among the Twelve, so a man called Stephen stood out among the Seven. He was a vigorous controversialist, and he incurred the suspicion of having uttered ' blasphemous words against Moses and God ' (Acts vi. 11). Like Jesus, he was accused of having spoken against the Temple : of having said that Jesus would overthrow this place and would change the customs which Moses handed down to the Jews. Acts vii. records a speech by Stephen in his defence, and in content and style alike it is so individual that we can hardly doubt that some memory of his attitude was preserved. Where Peter is represented as having attacked the Jewish authorities only in respect of their part in the death of Jesus, Stephen is made to deliver a frontal attack against the corporate conduct of Judaism throughout its history. He reverts to the freer critical attitude of Jesus, and appeals from the Jews to the words and actions of their God. Even Solomon's building of the temple is represented as an act of unfaithfulness to earlier ideals. Stephen was put to death, and there was a general persecution, in which the community (apart from the apostles, it is said) was scattered through Judaea and Samaria. This scattering produced missionary activity and the foundation of new groups, some of which Peter inspected. The extension of the mission to Samaritan territory was highly significant, for it involved the admissibility of Jewry's bitter foes to the Kingdom, but the most important new creation was the group at Antioch ; here the message was delivered to Gentiles also ; and here for many years Paul found his centre.

Whatever we think of the tradition according to which Paul was present at the stoning of Stephen, we cannot doubt that all serious persecution (including his) of the Christian movement takes its start from Stephen's activity. However eagerly James of Jerusalem and others maintained their personal loyalty to Judaism, and however respected James personally was in Jewish circles, what had now been said and done created enduring mistrust and hostility. Moderates on both sides might dislike this, but were powerless to check it : the antipathy excited by the disciples is made clear by the conduct of Herod Agrippa I, who in his brief reign used his powers to institute further persecution. For the young Pharisee Paul the case was clear. He had grown up in a deep sentimental attachment to the Temple and the Law and the People : to all that distinguished the Jew from those other races of men who were also God's children but who had refused the Law, had followed after strange gods and evil ways, had deserted the Temple, had flouted that minimal code which God had proclaimed to Noah (p. 114, later), and had treated God's People with brutal force or at best contemptuous indulgence. Now he must use all his powers and energy to resist an insidious form of national apostasy. So in the synagogues he stirs up the local authorities to employ the disciplinary methods at their power—scourging and excommunication at any rate. We do not know his age, but it is unlikely that a Jew would have taken a vigorous part in religious affairs before reaching thirty.

His work takes him to Damascus, and something happens to him. His own account is given in Gal. i. 11–21, where he is defending himself against opponents who criticized his teaching as derived from the Twelve at Jerusalem (and therefore, where discrepant, to be rejected : p. 162, later) : ' For I make known to you, brethren, that the Gospel preached by me is not after the fashion of men : for I did not [1] receive it from man nor was I taught it, but I had it through a revelation of Jesus Christ.' Then comes the reference to his earlier life quoted p. 32, above, and Paul continues : ' And when he who from my mother's womb had set me apart

[1] ' Any more than the Jerusalem Apostles ' is probably implied.

and through his grace called me, saw fit to reveal
his Son in me, in order that I might preach him
among the Gentiles, immediately I did not confer
with flesh and blood, nor did I go up to Jerusalem
to those who were Apostles before me, but I went
off to Arabia and returned again to Damascus.
Then after three years I went up to Jerusalem to
visit Cephas, and I remained with him fifteen days,
but I saw no other of the Apostles, save James the
brother of the Lord.   In what I write to you, lo,
before God, I do not lie.   Then I went to the parts
of Syria and Cilicia.'   The words ' I returned to
Damascus ' clearly imply that his conversion had
some relation to Damascus.   One other observation
must be made.   The phraseology echoes the call
of Jeremiah (i. 5) and the call of Isaiah (xlix. 1).
Paul at this time knew something of Christianity,
as an enemy, but he knew a great deal about the
prophets, as ideal types ; he felt himself as called
to their succession.   This helps us to understand
the enormous tolerance which he later showed to
other Christian prophets, even when he realized
that their inspirations needed control.   The call of
a prophet was not only to tell God's will, but also
to call men to do their part by penitence and right
conduct to fulfil a divine purpose.   Further, both
quotations from the Old Testament included a call
to the prophet to give a message which concerned the
' nations '—that is, to the Gentile world.

Acts gives three accounts of the conversion

(ix. 3–30, which includes the sequel; xxii. 4–21, with part of the sequel; xxvi. 10–18). In each Paul is journeying to Damascus on his errand of persecution, and, as he approaches the town, light from heaven blazes around him, and falling on the ground he hears a voice saying, ' Saul, Saul, why persecutest thou me ? '; and he replies, ' Who art thou ? '; and the voice answers, ' I am Jesus whom thou persecutest. Arise, and enter the city, and it shall be told thee what thou shalt do.' There are minor discrepancies, but the only major difference so far in the three versions is that in xxvi. 16–18 Jesus is made to give to Paul that commission to work among the Gentiles which he undoubtedly believed himself to have received direct from the risen Lord; in ix. 15 and xxii. 14 it was revealed to Ananias, and in xxii. 21 it was made explicit in the Temple (p. 83).

As the story continues, Paul entered Damascus led by the hand, for though his eyes were opened he saw not, and for three days he neither ate nor drank. Then a disciple in Damascus, named Ananias, being commanded by the Lord in a vision, came to him : his fears of visiting the persecutor having been allayed by the revelation that Paul was a vessel chosen to bear the Lord's name before nations and kings and the sons of Israel. Ananias laid his hands on Paul, saying that he was sent in order that Paul might receive his sight and be filled with the Holy Spirit; and Paul received his sight again, was baptized and took meat. Again, there is divergence in detail.

The reader will observe that in one crucial point this agrees with Paul's narrative. There is no word of Ananias *instructing* Paul in the truths of Christianity. Paul needs no instruction, although it is clear from Galatians that Paul's enemies said something of the sort. Paul could not fail to be fairly well acquainted with the tenets of the movement which he was persecuting, and after his conversion he must have made himself familiar with its traditions concerning Jesus ; at some time or other he must have learned these from the community at Damascus and supplemented his knowledge on the first of the two visits to Jerusalem which we shall consider later (p. 116). Nevertheless, the impulse of his conversion seemed to him to come from without, and he brought a wholly new spirit into the Christian Church. The Jerusalem disciples had grafted what they learned from Jesus, and their sentiments and reflections in relation to the risen Lord, on the Judaism in which they had been nurtured. Their religious lives had been enriched and changed, but without discontinuity. They never had to ' burn what they had adored and adore what they had burned '. For Paul, on the other hand, there was before his conversion a sharp antithesis between loyalty to Judaism on the one hand and the Christian movement on the other. His conversion happened as a drastic psychological crisis, which he does not and could not explain, and which we cannot either. Rom. vii. (p. 212, later) gives a generalized retrospect, written after many years. Paul here describes the morally neutral innocence of childhood,[1] followed by awareness of the Law, which not only invested any infractions of itself with a character of positive sinfulness, but also by its prohibitions, and in particular by its prohibition of desire, even stimulated to sin—somewhat, it has been remarked, like Adam's breach of the one command laid upon him. Paul tells also of an obsessional struggle in himself, his soul rejoicing in the Law, but another law in his limbs fighting against this and enslaving him.

Many critics have regarded this passage as in effect autobiography; others have held the ' I ' of the narrative to be a device of dramatization, and the experience described to be but the result of years of failure in preaching to Jews, and of concern for Gentile converts who needed to be protected against Judaizing propaganda. Both views contain elements of truth. Paul is not even trying to tell the story of his conversion, as Augustine and Newman told theirs, and he is not greatly interested in individual psychology. While recognizing differences of kind and of degree in spiritual gifts, here and elsewhere he is concerned with humanity as a whole in its relations to God and Law. All died in Adam; all

[1] Full responsibility for the keeping of the Law started at the age of thirteen.

can rise in Christ (p. 151, later). Any personal experience which Paul did not think a typical experience would be irrelevant : when he speaks of himself it is usually in unwilling self-defence, or by way of drawing moral inferences from the necessary conduct of a Christian teacher.

At the same time, we all tend to universalize what life has done to us, and Gal. ii. 19 shows that Paul was convinced that obedience to the Law had brought him to his later Christian position. Further, his whole contrast of the way of faith as set against works of the Law implies a conviction that the path of his youth was a wrong path and that any failures which he could recall were due not to personal shortcomings in his following of it, but to an intrinsic impossibility. That is not all ; in Galatians he asserts most solemnly that his Gospel came by revelation of Jesus Christ, and he implies that the universality of his teaching was part of it from the beginning—that, in fact, vocation and conversion were identical. Now memory is liable to foreshorten the course of events, and Paul may be doing this here ; but his statement seems to fit the facts of his character. Rebuffs from the Jewish compatriots to whom he addressed his message could perfectly well cause him to spend most of his time preaching to Gentiles ; but he was an inturned soul, absolutely sure of his revelation, wholly ready to be alone against the world and success or failure would hardly alter his basic convic-

tions. After all, his attitude towards the Law is
not one of gradual whittling away and compromis-
ing : it is radical rejection of the code as a way
which had failed and must fail. Had he been guided
purely by practical needs, it would have been easy
for him to incorporate the figure of Christ in
a liberalized Hellenistic Judaism. The so-called
Sibylline Oracles include various exhortations to
the heathen to give up murder, sexual sins, and
idolatry, to wash themselves, and to turn to God.
To this he could have added an emphasis on the
urgency of doing so at once on the guarantee of
forgiveness and deliverance by Christ, and he could
probably have made and accepted with the Jerusalem
church a compromise such as the ' Apostolic
Decrees ' (p. 113, later). Instead, he maintained
this elaborate theory which was hard to apply and
open to the gravest misunderstandings.

How could Paul hold the Law to have failed ?
The Law was the norm of a corporate religion
producing the corporate well-being of Israel ; it
prescribed conduct which was well-pleasing to God
and the Jew knew that such conduct was well-
pleasing *because* it had been revealed. Further,
since human nature is imperfect, the Law provided
sin-offerings and means of repentance. It was complete, and to very many, then and later, it provided
a wholly integrated and satisfying mode of life,
which enabled man to stand aright with God, if he
thought in a Palestinian way, or to live the good

life, if he thought in a Hellenistic way. Paul was a good Pharisee, irreproachable by Pharisee standards (Phil. iii. 6).

The point of difficulty for him perhaps lay in sexual desire, of which he speaks. Those who observed the Law were as conscious as other men of moral struggle, particularly of the struggle against sins of impurity in act and thought. These sins and many others were explained as being due to an ' evil instinct ' implanted in man (p. 167, later). Rabbinic teaching consistently maintained that the study of the Law [1] was the best antiseptic or way of diverting the mind from this and overcoming desire.

We possess in 4 Maccabees a speech given in a Jewish community of the Dispersion on the festival commemorating the re-dedication of the Temple, probably delivered in Paul's lifetime. Its theme is this concept stated in Hellenistic terms— that ' pious reasoning ', fortified by the instructions of the Law, can master all physical passions and weaknesses. We may imagine Paul as deeply possessed by this conviction, perhaps also as anxious about the sincerity of his resolves for amendment of life, without which repentance did not avail. His pride in the Law and in his observance of it (a pride which Rabbinic teachers recognized as a danger) might engender the sort of scrupulosity which any good Catholic confessor knows and can

[1] Sometimes coupled with work : *Otium, Catulle, tibi molestum est.*

handle. He probably could not have what we call good ' spiritual direction '. Further, he may have been influenced by individuals or groups obsessed with a gloomy view of human sinfulness and an anxiety concerning man's state such as we find in 4 Esdras. Apocalyptic ideas were certainly in the air ; and such ideas commonly gave a prominent place to the conception of a present depravity which could be remedied only by divine action. ' I will create in them a holy spirit ' (Book of Jubilees i. 23). The new purity, like the new life of the dead, would come from God ; meanwhile man and the universe were marked by evil.

The mental components of Paul the Christian were the same as the mental components of Paul the Jew. The germ of his universalism could easily have been in him from early days. Judaism was universal as well as national. The desire to preserve morality and monotheism by the unremitting observance of the Law and the legacy of hatred which the Maccabee struggle bequeathed to posterity caused the national aspect to predominate. Nevertheless, the universalism of Isaiah, which Paul echoes in Rom. x., was not forgotten, and it was held that God loved all his children, even those who had strayed very far in foolishness. Perhaps in youth at Tarsus Paul had been struck by that presence of moral virtues in Gentiles of which he speaks in Rom. ii. 14 and wished to spread that light which as a Jew he claimed to have (ibid. ii. 19–20). Certainly, Gamaliel belonged to the more liberal trend in belief.

Paul was a natural extremist, and he took an extreme view of the claim that the Anointed One of God was to be found in the person of a criminal handed over by the religious authorities of the nation to the Romans to die what could be regarded as an accursed death (Gal. iii. 13), the more so when this claim was by Stephen coupled with provocative criticisms of the whole of Jewish religious history and with what seemed to be impious words about the Temple. Paul could not treat this movement with polite indifference or contempt as something ephemeral which would run its course. Further, analogies suggest that his conversion was not the sudden thing which it seemed to him : the movement had probably fascinated him at the same time that it excited his deepest animosity, and it must have been the question, if the unvoiced question, of his life for some time. ' Why dost thou kick against the pricks ? ' is the truth of psychology, if not of history. On the face of it, Christianity was not only wrong but enigmatic. Paul might hate the ways of the Sadducees, but he could understand them : he may have thought the Essenes eccentric, but he probably respected them as carrying to an extreme the Pharisaic ideal of purity : he probably disapproved of the revolutionary anti-Roman extremists, but he could fully comprehend indignation over the oppression of Sion. This on the other hand was illogical, incomprehensible; and that Stephen should die for it, as readily as Pharisees had died rather than fail to protest against Herod's defiance of the Law, was the height of illogicality.

Paul's conversion meant for him the recognition that the condemned criminal was in fact the Anointed One of God, living now in the glory of the Spirit world, and that through this Anointed One an imperious call to tell the good tidings had come to him, Paul. This was a sudden intuition; thereafter Paul had to readjust his whole thinking. The death of Jesus was the outcome of the Jewish life by the Law as practised; it was not the mistake of individuals, but the climax of a chain of errors (1 Thess. ii. 15), not an unfortunate incident, but the critical hour of history. It involved a fresh searching of the Scriptures.

Paul did not, like the early converts after Pentecost, join the Way; as he saw it, he was, so to speak, physically taken by the Lord. The call was a personal call. Nevertheless, it was a call to the service of a holy nation—as in Rom. ix. 25 he quotes from Hos. ii. 25, ' I will call as my people the people that was not mine, and as my beloved her that was not '; the ' sons of Abraham ' who owed their sonship to faith. This principle of faith was found by Paul above all in two familiar texts, Gen. xv. 6 and Hab. ii. 4, which came into his mind as he sought to relate his new experience to the old revelation. The emphasis on faith, meaning both trust and faithfulness, was strong in contemporary Judaism, although it was not there put in antithesis to the performance of works of the Law and could almost seem to be itself a work. The view, of which Paul makes so much, that Abraham was its hero was familiar. Paul had but to develop this and to give it the peculiar linking to Christ and through Christ to God which corresponded to his own experience. This new people of God were related to God through Christ and related to Christ with peculiar intimacy. *Dikaiosyne*, ' righteousness ', that is, primarily ' standing right with God ', acceptance by God, was theirs by a free gift, not depending on Israel's past or man's intention, nor again supplementing the righteousness which men had already, but wholly new, the fruit of a passivity which was the source of a new energy in action. The contrast with Paul's earlier quest of holiness is the contrast between the surgical removal of an ulcer and its daily draining and disinfection.

This way of life differs not only from that of the Pharisees, but also from that of Jesus. The Pharisees also made faith a cardinal virtue, but they believed in a continual struggle to do God's will. This depended on man : ' Everything is in the power of Heaven except the fear of Heaven.' Now Hellenistic Judaism shows something like a doctrine of grace, while Rabbinic Judaism has traces of the idea that God protected the feet of the pious and that the Spirit (or Shekinah, that is, presence) of

God upheld the righteous ; furthermore, the regular prayers of the synagogue, like many of the Psalms, asked for moral blessings before all else. Nevertheless, the saying just quoted represents the dominant idea. God sent prophets and by warnings and chastisements tried to bring man to repent, and again helped every movement of man's heart towards him, but the responsibility and initiative rested with man. Redemption was self-redemption, under God and with the use of the means which he had provided.

Jesus taught a more natural and simple ethic in which man could prepare for the Kingdom by choosing voluntarily a given type of action and a given type of life ; God would give to him all he needed (Matt. vii. 7 ff. ; Luke xi. 9 ff.), with a bountifulness which corresponded to the Pauline *charis*, ' grace '. Paul's vision of man in relation to God is a more complex one, but in the daily problems of life he never abandoned it, although at all times he had to teach that man must do his part under grace to enjoy the fruits of the righteousness imputed to him, and to become what ideally he was. The moral responsibility of the individual was not destroyed, but sharpened.

So Paul introduced a revolutionary principle of ethics. On the face of it, he had parted company with Judaism ; and it is quite natural that we should ask whether his new point of view is not to be explained from influences arising from the Hellenistic world of thought. Many excellent scholars have so interpreted Paul's view of the believer's identity with Christ and his doctrines of the Spirit, of baptism, and of the Eucharist. Certainly Paul and the Christians of Antioch, with whom he was in close contact during the earlier years of his life in the Church, were exposed to non-Jewish trends of thought and life, and we can almost certainly see the product of such contacts in the practical ethical directions which Paul gave to his converts. Since, however, Jewish eschatological presuppositions were certainly the starting-point of Paul's Christianity, and since his theology and sacramentalism can be explained in terms of them, we are bound to prefer that explanation. The differences between Pauline and Hellenistic sacramentalism are essential and not superficial, and the concept, sometimes invoked, of a general Hellenistic sacramentalism as a substantial entity in the thought of the time is not warranted by the existing evidence. The Hellenistic influences which reached Paul reached him mainly through hellenized Jewish milieus.

In any case, Paul's unconscious presuppositions and instincts remained Jewish. While he rejected the Law as a code the validity of which was now superseded by the new and yet old way of faith,[1]

[1] We should not explain this from the fact that Paul regarded the Kingdom as having in a sense come with Jesus ; for the Law was to remain in full vigour during the days of the Messiah.

at the same time the total revelation of the Old Testament remained the supreme authority ; Paul interpreted it in the light of what he had now learned, but no Pharisee was bound to any theory of literal interpretation.   The call of Abraham and God's promise to his children were fundamental ; the ethical commands were assumed, and Paul probably found it hard to understand why so many of his Gentile converts lacked the moral instinct fostered by the Law.   The Jew retained a priority before God ; the ' merits of the Patriarchs ' remained, even if with a different nuance.   Further, the guidance of the Spirit was to be controlled by common sense (p. 198, later).   The Jewish concept of merit and demerit did not disappear ; God would reckon the good and evil deeds of individuals at the Judgment (1 Cor. iii. 15 ; Rom. ii. 5).   Again, Paul, as was natural in a once zealous Pharisee, adopted counsels of perfection which he would not impose upon all (1 Cor. vii. 8-9).   We must not seek to press the Pauline view into any scheme of logical consistency.   Yet it has a freshness and an originality of a high order : ' We are nearing new heights, and I perceive that the way up is not merely a path but verily a part of whatever height is reached.'

At the centre was Christ. Jesus was Lord (*Maran*, ' our Lord ') to the Jerusalem Christians ; he stood between God and them, and his activity, past and present, included all that differentiated the time in which they were living from the whole of previous human history. *Maran* was perhaps originally no more than a courtesy title describing the Master to whom the disciples felt intimately related, although even at Jerusalem it was perhaps associated with Ps. cx. When the term was hellenized, the natural word was *Kyrios*, and that was a constant predicate of God in the Septuagint. Paul did not shrink from the inference. He held, indeed, that vocation was primarily from God and that the relation of Jesus to God was and remained one of subordination, but he held also that this subordination was temporarily in abeyance. God had given to Jesus the name of *Kyrios* (Phil. ii. 9–11), to show that divine power for the salvation of men was concentrated in Jesus ; to be able to call Jesus *Kyrios*, as also to believe in his resurrection, was the condition of deliverance (Rom. x. 9). Lordship was the essential quality of Jesus, and divine operations are described in terms either of God or of Christ : ' the tribunal of God ' (Rom. xiv. 10) is identical with ' the tribunal of Christ ' (2 Cor. v. 10) ; ' the love of Christ ' (Rom. viii. 35) is identical with ' the love of God in Christ Jesus our Lord ' (Rom. viii. 39), and ' the love of God poured forth in our hearts by the Holy Spirit because of Christ's death ' (Rom. v. 5 f.). Again, ' faith towards God ' (1 Thess. i. 8) is parallel to ' faith towards Christ ' (Col. ii. 5) ; God's glory is seen in Christ's face (2 Cor. iv. 6). We find also ' the churches of Christ ' (Rom. xvi. 16), ' the churches in Christ '

(Gal. i. 22), ' the church of God ' (1 Cor. i. 2, etc.), ' an apostle . . . through Jesus Christ and God the Father ' (Gal. i. 1).

That is not all. ' The Spirit of God ', ' the Spirit of Christ ', ' Christ within you ', all seem to describe the same thing, although in Rom. viii. the Spirit has an independent activity. Just as Israel became for Paul a spiritualized universal concept, so also he emphasized the universality of Christ. The very fact that, as was natural in Greek, the term Christ became more a name than a title, is symbolical of a fundamental change. The prophetic framework is the background for a dynamic force released by the Cross. It is very striking that Paul so seldom uses the actual phrase ' forgiveness of sins '; the idea is in his mind, but he is filled with the idea of the positive creative activity of Christ within the individual soul and within the community of souls. This community of souls in the Church had for Paul an aspect which was somewhat different from that which it wore in the eyes of the Jerusalem community. Christ and the Spirit were everything; unlimited deference could be shown to the older disciples as a matter of charity, but no obedience could be yielded to them as a matter of authority. Jerusalem could claim respect and grateful benefaction, but not obedience. We shall see the working out of this principle in Paul's life.

How quickly Paul elaborated these views we cannot say. In any case, he did elaborate them as a personal system. We cannot hope to recover the processes by which he reached them; what has been here attempted is only to suggest considerations which from our knowledge of the times could conceivably have been in his mind.

CHAPTER IV

PAUL'S EARLIER CHRISTIAN PERIOD

THE years following Paul's conversion lie in a darkness pierced by few gleams of light. We have seen what Gal. i. 17 tells us ; an immediate journey into Arabia (that is to say, the kingdom of Nabataea governed from Petra by Aretas IV, who was one of the minor royalties who lived on the fringe of the Roman Empire), a return to Damascus, a visit to Jerusalem three [1] years after his conversion, for fifteen days, and activity in the parts of Syria and Cilicia. Then ' after 14 years ', [2] presumably counted from the first visit to Jerusalem, the famous second visit which we shall have to consider later (p. 105). One piece of detail is afforded us by 2 Cor. xi. 32–3 : ' In Damascus the ethnarch of King Aretas was watching the city of the Damascenes to catch me, and I was lowered in a basket through a window in the wall and escaped from

---

[1] Which may, on the ancient habit of inclusive reckoning, mean ' after 2 years '.

[2] On the same principle, perhaps meaning ' after 13 years '.

his hands.' Aretas can hardly, as some think, have held Damascus : but his officer, called an ethnarch —who may have been the head of the doubtless substantial group of Nabataeans resident in Damascus and in its territory—was waiting to hurry Paul over the frontier, in the hope that if he were caught and executed, Rome might not ask questions ; such risks were taken.

Acts ix. 19–30 gives a different story. There Paul, after his recovery of sight and his baptism, preached in the synagogues of Damascus that Jesus was Son of God. This unexpected activity of the man known as a persecutor excited considerable attention, and the Jews plotted to kill him : this became known to him, but the Jews watched the gates day and night to destroy him ; so the disciples let him down from the wall in a basket, and he went to Jerusalem and tried to attach himself to the church there. Its members were all afraid of him, not trusting his conversion ; but Barnabas took him to the Apostles and related his vision on the road to Damascus and his bold preaching in Damascus. Paul taught for a while in Jerusalem ; but another plot was made against his life, and the brethren conducted him to Caesarea and shipped him to Tarsus. Acts xxii. 17 gives yet another version in which, when Paul has returned to Jerusalem—on the face of it, as in Acts ix, quite soon after his conversion—and was praying in the Temple, he fell into an ecstasy and saw a man who said to him : ' Speed, and leave Jerusalem in haste, for they will not receive thy testimony concerning Me '; the visitant, and it was the Lord, later said : ' Go, for I shall send thee afar among the Gentiles.'

The writer of Acts shows no clear acquaintance with Paul's letters,[1] and for this part of Paul's life he had no information comparable with that which was at his disposal for the missionary journeys. It would seem that all he knew is of a hurried departure by Paul from Damascus to save his life, of a brief visit to Jerusalem, and of a journey to Cilicia—without details. We have the advantage of reading what Paul says, but we cannot settle various questions : did Paul follow Old Testament precedents and retire into the desert for contemplation ? If that was all, how did he attract the attention of the Nabataean authorities ? Did he preach in Arabia after the solitude which Gal. i. 16 suggests ? If so, was the official of Aretas acting as a result of conflict between Paul and the Jews or the civil authority in Arabia ? Or did conflict arise in Damascus, where there was a big Jewish colony,

---

[1] Individual linguistic echoes—which may be due to some intermediary source or to oral tradition—do not affect the main point, which is that a man who had read the Pauline Epistles could not have written Acts xv. (p. 116, later).

and was the official acting to please the Jews of Judaea and secure their eventual support for Aretas ? The probability is that Paul engaged in some missionary activity, as the unescapable consequence of his conversion, and that it provoked opposition without attaining important results. In any case, the objection that he could not make himself understood to Arabs who did not speak Greek is invalid ; the difference between Palestinian Aramaic and Nabataean was not more than one of dialect. The important certainty is that two or three years after conversion Paul is active in the mission, and concerned to establish personal relationships with the leaders of the Church at Jerusalem.

The thirteen or fourteen years ' in parts of Syria and Cilicia ' must have been of supreme importance in Paul's evolution : for during them he was engaged in missionary activity to Gentiles and he had need and time to develop his personal theology and his technique of preaching and argument. Some development can be traced in his extant Epistles, but it is more a matter of self-adjustment to situations ; the main personal evolution lies before the years to which they belong. Our knowledge of the other events of these years is in effect limited to two facts. First, Acts xi., after describing the origin of the Christian community in Antioch and the preaching of the Word to Gentiles there (p. 63, above), relates how word of all this came to the ears of the church of Jerusalem, and Barnabas was sent to inspect. Here, as in Peter's tour or visit to the communities founded by Philip in Samaria, the Jerusalem church shows a definite will to control. Communities, wherever they were founded, could individually be called *ekklesiai*, churches; but at the same time there was one *ekklesia*, one totality of the Elect who had already sealed their election. On this point Paul, as his theology developed, was at one with the Twelve and James. Where they were to part company was on the fact that the Twelve and James claimed a primacy for Jerusalem and a right to give advice which could not be disregarded. We may for once go beyond the chronological limits of this book and observe that in effect the Jerusalem principle triumphed, but with the inclusion of Paul in the group whose names guaranteed the traditions of the churches which claimed descent from them. The primacy after 70 rested indeed not with Jerusalem, for the war had scattered the congregation and its remains dwindled into insignificance, but with local churches which could claim foundation by an Apostle (that is, now, one of the Twelve or Paul), and more and more with Rome in particular. Such authority became the test of Catholic orthodoxy. But the principle of authority itself is primitive Christian, and takes its origin in the designation by

Jesus of the Twelve for their functions in the Kingdom (p. 49, above).

Vital issues were at stake and were to arise continually through Paul's life. Could a Gentile acquire through baptism the right to a share in the life of the World to Come, without submitting to circumcision, and so becoming an adopted Jew? And, even if he could, were Jewish Christians to eat and drink with him, and disregard the impurity which such conduct involved from a Jewish standpoint? According to Acts x., Peter had accepted the indications that the Roman centurion Cornelius and those with him had received the Spirit, as evidence of their belonging in effect to the Church, and baptized them: but if the story is historical, that might have been the recognition of a special dispensation; in any case, the controversy was far from settled. Development was natural: uncircumcised men were baptized at Antioch. At Rome they probably formed a majority by the time that Paul wrote his Epistle, and it seems clear that they did not observe the Law. The banishment of Jews in 49 had perhaps contributed to this: but it may be regarded as largely a natural process arising out of the tendency to freedom inherent in the movement. Paul did not originate freedom from the Law: what he did was to give it a positive meaning.

The preaching of the Word at Antioch to Gentiles at least required scrutiny. Barnabas was sent as apostolic delegate and ' arriving and seeing the gracious power of God, rejoiced and encouraged them all to remain in the purpose of their hearts true to the Lord, for Barnabas was a good man and full of the Holy Spirit and faith. And a considerable multitude was added to the Lord '. So Barnabas approved, and went to Tarsus and brought Paul to Antioch, where the two lived in its church for a year and taught a considerable multitude, and the disciples were there first called Christians. This means that Barnabas knew of Paul as an active preacher in this kind of missionary enterprise ; and brought him to Antioch, and the two became the dominant spirits in the community. Barnabas thus provided Paul with a much more important base of operations, in the third city of the Empire, which had a very important Jewish community (said to make many proselytes), and also gave him the companionship which Paul so deeply valued.

The other fact of these years comes from 2 Cor. xii. 2. Paul is there answering opponents who were disposed to underrate his authority on the ground that he did not have a spiritual experience—in the fully supernatural sense—as rich and deep as theirs. He says, ' I know a man in Christ fourteen years ago—whether in the body, I do not know, or whether apart from the body, I do not know, God knows: I know such an one to have been carried to the third heaven. And I know of such an one—whether in the body, or apart from the body, I do not know: God knows—that he was carried into Paradise and heard unspeakable words, which a man may not utter. I will boast on behalf of such an one, but I will not boast on my own behalf, save in my weakness.' The recipient of the vision is Paul: he is using, for a very deliberate purpose, a circumlocution like the Aramaic ' this man '. He is speaking of a time within this period, and describing some inward consciousness of an experience like that which is ascribed to Old Testament worthies in apocryphal documents; four Rabbis were said to have had the like privilege. But the hesitant words are in striking contrast with the glib literary conventions of much vision-literature, Jew and Greek alike. Whatever we make of such language, Paul's absolute conviction that he had received such experience, and above all that he had been called to his new faith by a direct personal appearance of the Lord, did more than anything else give him heart of courage to meet the adversaries of whom we shall hear so much. In the last analysis, he knew that his sufficiency was of God, and no defeat or temporary depression could give him the self-pity of a disappointed man.

Barnabas and Paul were active men in an active community, and the harvest of the Gentile mission in Antioch and perhaps in Tarsus seemed to justify a new missionary offensive. Hitherto deliberate missionary activity had been confined to Palestine and neighbouring territory and Tarsus. The Gospel of Jesus had spread to Alexandria and Rome, and doubtless to many minor centres ; but, so far as we know, simply through the migration of individuals and of ideas, not through deliberate propagation. Acts xiii. 1–3 introduces the new departure with appropriate solemnity : ' There were at Antioch in the church there prophets and teachers, Barnabas and Symeon who was also called Niger and Lucius of Cyrene, and Manaen the foster-brother of Herod the tetrarch and Saul. And as they were serving the Lord and fasting the Holy Spirit spoke : " Separate for me Barnabas and Saul unto the work to which I have called them." Then (the brethren) after fasting and praying and laying hands upon them sent them forth.'

Taking with them John Mark, a young Christian from the community at Jerusalem, they sailed to Cyprus. Barnabas was a Cypriot by birth, and he might hope to be able to operate on familiar soil with knowledge of local conditions and a better chance of success. We read that he and Paul preached in the synagogue at Salamis, and that Paul worsted a magician in the entourage of the Roman governor, and converted the governor ; but the story reads like an acted parable of the conquest of magic by Christianity rather than a record of fact. From Paphos the missionaries sailed to Perga, on the opposite coast of Asia Minor. John left them, and they proceeded to Pisidian Antioch, where Paul preached in the synagogue and made a considerable impression on those who heard him, Jews and proselytes alike. His first teaching in such a community would probably be—as Acts represents it—identical with that of Peter, the proof from Old Testament prophecy that the recently crucified Jesus was the Anointed One so long foretold, and the exhortation of his hearers to avail themselves of this new possibility of securing the remission of sins. On the next sabbath, we read, almost the whole city came to hear—(just as they would have flocked to hear a wandering lecturer, as later Dion of Prusa or Lucian : interesting visitors at Pisidian Antioch were probably few), and the Jews were filled with envy and contradicted what Paul said. Paul replied that he would turn to the Gentiles, and the Word spread. Preaching in the synagogue till it was made difficult or impossible, followed by direct teaching of Gentiles, is a regular formula in Acts, and probably represents Paul's policy. He thought of himself, and was thought of, as primarily the Apostle to the Gentiles ; and his greatest success was no doubt attained among Gentiles ; but it is natural to suppose that he acted on the doctrine of the prior right of the Jew which he expresses in Romans (p. 78, above) and in the synagogues he would find the most sympathetic pagans. On this occasion, just as on others later, the Jews made continued residence in the city impossible for the missionaries, and they moved on to Iconium.

Here we have the same sequence : preaching in the synagogue, winning of many Jews and Gentiles, Jewish hatred and Jewish stirring up of Gentile opposition.[1] The conflict at Antioch is represented as more acute and as dividing the city into two camps—those who were for the Jews and those who were for the missionaries. At the end there was a general move to stone Paul and Barnabas, and they fled to Lystra and Derbe in Lycaonia and preached there. Acts proceeds to give a vignette of the missionary in purely Gentile surroundings, as a counterpart to the pictures just given of the missionary in a predominantly Jewish environment. Paul healed a cripple, and the multitudes seeing what he had done lifted up their voices in the Lycaonian language, saying, ' The gods have come down to us in the likeness of men,' and called Barnabas

---

[1] Acts repeatedly represents the opening stages of a Pauline mission as not exciting antipathy—e.g. at Corinth (xviii. 4) ; the trial mission at Ephesus (xviii. 20) is so described.

(who presumably had the more dignified appearance) Zeus, and Paul, since he was the chief speaker, Hermes (who was the god of speech). Then the priest of the temple of Zeus before the city brought bulls and fillets to the gates, and together with the crowds would fain offer sacrifice to Barnabas and Paul. They, when they heard of this, rent their garments (the traditional Jewish way of expressing horror of blasphemous acts and words) and ran into the crowd, and passionately implored them to stop, saying: 'O men, why do you do these things? We too are human beings subject to the same experiences as you are' (that is, not ageless and deathless, as gods were supposed to be), 'giving you the good news that you should turn from these foolish things to the living God, who made the heaven and the earth and the sea and all that in them is, who in past generations allowed all races to walk in their own ways—although He did not leave Himself without a witness, doing good, giving you from heaven rains and fruitful seasons, and filling your hearts with food and gladness.' In spite of saying this, they barely restrained the crowds from doing sacrifice to them. Then Jews came from Antioch and Iconium, stoned Paul, dragged him out of the city, and left him for dead.

Let us consider some of the implications of this story and of the general presuppositions of

Paul's advance into Gentile territory. The writer
of Acts indicates that this is a backward community, in which the populace talks its native
language. All over the Near East the language
of cultivated men was Greek. Roman officials
and Roman colonies used also Latin for formal
purposes, but did not confine themselves to it
even for them. Native languages belonged to
the uncultivated folk and above all to country
dwellers. Christianity now and for long spread
in urban centres, linked by roads; and the two
phenomena, of a language intelligible nearly everywhere and of communications leading to all cities
easily and with considerable safety from brigandage
were of paramount importance for missionary
work.

The dissemination of Greek was due to the
conquests of Alexander the Great. Between 336
and 323 B.C. he became master of the whole of
the Persian Empire—Asia Minor, Syria, Mesopo-
tamia, Egypt, Persia, and the Western fringe of
India. After his death his conquests were divided
among his generals, but most remained thereafter
within the Greek cultural area, and the use of
the Greek language was the badge and the pledge
of political and economic advantage as well as
of educational superiority. The notion that the
essence of being a Greek was cultural rather
than racial had been voiced earlier; now it was
translated into effective reality, without the Greeks

to any material degree abandoning their personal pride in purity of stock.

In religion the Greek element was for the most part not an antithesis but a complement of the native element, acting in a measure as a solvent and a cause of modification; political changes, whereby many temple-estates passed into Imperial possession, also contributed to this tendency. The one important opposition to Hellenism at this time was Judaism, in which the national basis resisted assimilation, above all after the attempt of Antiochus Epiphanes to accelerate such tendencies had called forth the passionate revolt of the Maccabees. Elsewhere native gods were called by Greek names—Zeus, Hermes, Artemis, Apollo and the like—sometimes with the addition of local epithets indicating the homes of the deities so described. Inscriptions show that Zeus and Hermes were worshipped in Lycaonia, but we do not know whether they were Greek gods or native gods in a Greek linguistic dress, and the second supposition is the more probable. Nevertheless, we must not underestimate the vitality of purely Greek worships in this expansion of Hellenism. The Greek gods were the gods consecrated by Greek literature and Greek art: so were some Oriental gods who had been drawn within the Greek cultural ambit during and before the earlier part of the Hellenistic age—Adonis, Cybele, Isis and Sarapis. Other Oriental gods were liable to be regarded by cultivated men as more or less barbarian. Further, some Greek gods, as represented in literature and art, had connotations with an emotional content which was more than purely cultural. The majestic figure of Zeus served as a symbol, effective because it was traditional, for a widespread trend towards the idea of a god supreme over all other gods, acting in the universe through minor deities who were his servants or effluences. Heracles, the Dioscuri, and Dionysus were types of divine privilege attained by a canonization for services to mankind, for purging the earth of evil and spreading the blessings of civilization and giving help and succour now, as of old, to men in need; so was Asclepius, the god of healing. Dionysus, further, had something of his old meaning as the god of enthusiasm, the god of the cult in which the worshipper (as in the choruses of the *Bacchae* of Euripides) transcended the limitations of his humanity; in Asia Minor under the Empire, he was worshipped by more private guilds than any other god.

The city of Rome, after various hesitancies, finally undertook the control of most of the legacy of Alexander west of the Euphrates. This political change was not attended by cultural consequences comparable with Rome's work in her Western province. In Spain, Gaul, Africa, Germany, Britain, and in the Danube region, Rome created and fostered the epoch-making development which we call Romanization. In the Near East, Rome administered and controlled, but for the most part did not create. Apart from the Julian calendar as locally adapted, the one substantial novelty was that the ruler of Rome, the First Citizen or *princeps*, who held effectively absolute power by a series of constitutional devices and fictions but was from the standpoint of the Near East simply Caesar or King, universally took the place of various local rulers. He was a superman. His personal idiosyncrasies would be known, and admired or mocked in Rome; here unless, like Trajan or Hadrian, he was a great traveller, they faded into the nimbus which surrounded his position. It had long been customary to build temples and offer sacrifices to rulers in the Near East; now such honours were paid to the Emperor—oaths were taken by his *genius*, the divinity in him or with him, and sacrifices and prayers and ceremonies and dedications of buildings beyond number were made in his honour. The issue of Imperial power is not raised in Acts until Paul and Silas are at Thessalonica, where their accusers say (xvii. 7), ' And all these men act contrary to the decrees of Caesar, saying that there is another king, Jesus.' That may be part of the artistry of the book; perhaps, however, in the fifth decade of the first century, Roman power was not yet so important in men's minds in a backward region, except in any Roman colonies which it contained.

Two other general phenomena of the contemporary world figure in Acts—magic and philosophy. Paul has a contest with the sorcerer Elymas in Cyprus, and we hear later of Jewish exorcists at Ephesus who use the name of Jesus to expel evil spirits, and end by being roughly handled by one, and of Ephesian converts who, on becoming Christians, make a bonfire of their magical books. Attempts to control the course of nature in such ways were common. The average man, if you could have persuaded him to tell you his idea of how things happened, would probably have replied something like this. Most things happen as they must—that is fate, whether conceived vaguely, or more definitely thought to be written in or by the stars in their courses; and we sometimes try to know what is going to happen by consulting an oracle, where we put questions to a god through his prophet, or a person inspired in some way or other, like the slave-girl at Philippi in Acts xvi. 16, or a dead man raised for the purpose by someone who knows a formula which will compel him to appear and answer. Nevertheless, there are beings called gods who have supreme power. The way in which things normally happen is piously supposed to represent their general will; but individual gods may be persuaded to intervene on our behalf, and cause this or that thing to go as we wish it, if we persuade them by prayers and sacrifices, or promises of sacrifices, or vigorous demonstrations, either of our sorrow for actions which may have given them offence, or of our gratitude for what we conceive to be past favours of theirs. If they are gods in connection with whose worships there are initiatory rites, whereby we are reborn to a new life under their protection, then of course we can look for very special help ; but such ceremonies are expensive and often cannot be undertaken without some omen or dream to indicate that the would-be initiate is acceptable as a candidate ; and of course some of the most accessible of these initiations do not make any promises except for your security in the after-life. Yet there are other ways of getting your wishes in ordinary matters. You go to a man called a magician, *magos*—not minding the supercilious folk who call him a humbug, *goês* —and you ask him to help you. If it is some sickness from which you suffer or which you fear, he will take a very precious book and for the relevant fee copy out a spell and inscribe it on something which you can hang round your neck. He can even give you a spell to wear in the same way which will guarantee you against all sorts of perils, physical and otherwise, and promise you success in love and every kind of success in your small world. If you wish to secure the affections of a particular woman, he will give you a spell to bury under her threshold. If you wish to cause someone to die or sicken, there is a spell for that. In each case you get ' the words which make wished-for things happen ' (to use the phrase whereby the Iglulik Eskimos describe their magical formulas). These words are invocations to various deities, Egyptian, Greek, Jewish, Babylonian, and there are invocations so powerful that, like initiation, they convey a new status and make you of the character of the immortals. With such, and with some others, you must combine certain fastings and other additional measures.

Philosophy has been mentioned as one of the interests of Tarsus. In the first century of the Empire, while there were still some who pursued not only metaphysical quests but also those considerations of physical science which then fell within the scope of philosophy (so that, till a generation or so ago, we still spoke of Natural Philosophy), the name philosophy meant for most men the study of how we should live : it was predominantly ethical. The serious consideration of philosophical questions formed the part of education which corresponded to University studies to-day, and was commonly pursued at centres like Athens, Alexandria, Rome and Tarsus, which corresponded to Universities ; but also in various ways—through books, through travelling lecturers, through the Cynics who talked in city streets to all who would hear them—some notions of this art of living reached wider circles and, more than most things of the time, corresponded to what to-day we call ' personal religion '. Many philosophers took an interest in cult and myth, and, in so far as pagan cult and myth assume a theological character, it is by the application of philosophical speculations.

To return to what happened at Lystra, the enthusiastic gesture of the inhabitants may arrest our attention. But similar gestures of adoration are common in the literature of the time : Cornelius offers it to Peter in Acts x. 25 and Peter replies, ' I too am a man.' Here it gives the setting for a brief sermon to Gentiles. Paul cannot speak about the Old Testament or the argument from prophecy ; and if he told them that Jesus was the Messiah they would be no wiser for that. He has to attack idolatry, as any advocate of Judaism would, and like such an advocate argues in effect—(if we may fill out the very brief summary here from the speech at Athens in Acts xvii.)—that God's existence is shown by his acts of goodness and loving-kindness. The peculiar and Christian element in the speech is the insistence that a change of heart is *now* necessary ; because (and again Acts xvii. supplies what is lacking) God is about to judge the world.

After the attack Paul and Barnabas proceeded to Derbe, where they are said to have taught successfully. Their return journey by Lystra, Iconium, Antioch is marked by exhortation of the new disciples and by the establishment of an ecclesiastical organization. So they voyage back to Antioch and there is general satisfaction that a door of faith had been opened to the Gentiles.

A great step had indeed been taken. From the standpoint of many at Jerusalem it was not so clear that it was a step forward. If they had shut their eyes or had given a more or less reluctant approval to developments at Antioch itself, they were not necessarily prepared to see Gentile communities well on the way to outnumber Jewish Christians.[1] It might be that the sayings of Jesus implied that those places in the number of the Elect which Jews were unwilling to take should be opened to Gentiles ; but an admission, nay an eager invitation to Gentiles *en masse*, was another story. Let them be circumcised and accept the Jewish Law, and add the promises of Christ and the gift of the Spirit. This did not seem an impossible aspiration ; the Sabbath was kept by many and the food-laws by some who did not come to the point of circumcision, and circumcision could be the logical consequence.

[1] It may well be that the newer adherents at Jerusalem included some stricter Jews.

Such was the sincere conviction of many at Jerusalem, who had found the Law comfortable and regarded it as the divine safeguard of right conduct; their faith in Christ was essential to them, but so also was their membership of Israel, and in Israel national feeling was already gathering force for the fatal explosion of 66.

Paul could not concede this. It was not because certain Jews had earlier held that for a Gentile the abandonment of idolatry and the acceptance of the moral code of Judaism was enough, and the assumption of proselyte status unnecessary; for while, on the liberal theory, such conduct would suffice to secure a share of the life of the World to Come, it did not remove the Jew's scruples against enjoying table-fellowship with the Gentile. Modern writers have spoken of such Gentiles—from whom the Christian missions recruited many members—as 'the fringe of the synagogue'. But for Paul there could be no 'fringe of the Church'; for him you were 'in Christ' or you were not 'in Christ' (p. 149): there was no half-way house, and there were no second-best Christians.[1] His whole posi-

---

[1] This is clear, in spite of the fact that there were counsels of perfection (1 Cor. vii. 8–9), a higher theology available for those who were qualified to receive it (1 Cor. iii. 1 ff.), and a possibility of continual spiritual growth (Phil. iii. 12 ff.: cf. the metaphor 'edify', which is literally 'build up').

tion turned on this; for him, as we have seen, there was a real antithesis between pre-Christian life and Christian life; and the 'fruits of the Spirit' which for thirteen years he had seen in Gentile converts were for him irrefutable evidence. No doubt Paul as a Jew did not find the Law burdensome. Our evidence on Jewish attitudes towards the Law comes from idealizing accounts, but it seems that, although the phrase 'the yoke of the Law' was common, and some of the relatively ignorant in Galilee and elsewhere regarded Pharisaic minutiae as a burden, the majority of Jews, and certainly of Pharisees, thought of the Law as a privilege and not a burden. Paul after his conversion obeyed the Law, though he mingled freely with the Gentiles and had table-fellowship with them—presumably without employing those subsequent purifications which custom imposed. Nevertheless, from his changed standpoint, he could very well think of the Law as a tremendous burden which had been removed. Moreover, he must have realized that, if circumcision was made a *sine qua non*, conversion of male Gentiles would thereby be limited in numbers; the practice was regarded as one of the odd habits of Jews, and the frequentation of public baths precluded secrecy.

The Jewish Christians at Antioch seem to have made no difficulties about the freest fellowship with Gentile converts,[1] and Paul no doubt had come to regard such intercourse as a matter which was outside the range of controversy. The Jewish Christians at Jerusalem must have been aware of these conditions, but had probably more or less ignored them, perhaps treating them as a local phenomenon which might be regarded as a special case. Now they could no longer maintain this attitude, for the missionary success of Paul and his associates looked as though it could create a serious counterpoise to their own type of religious life. We have an account of part of the controversy written by Paul himself at a later date, when emissaries from Jerusalem tried to persuade Paul's Galatian converts to follow what they regarded as a more excellent way (Gal. ii. 1 ff. ; for brevity some explanations of this very difficult passage are added in square brackets). ' Then after fourteen years I went up again to Jerusalem, with Barnabas, taking with me Titus also [Titus was there as a subordinate] ; and I went up in accordance with a revelation [i.e., not as a result of orders to come and explain myself, and not in natural submission to my ecclesiastical superiors, which I do not recognize them to be]. I set forth to them, and, privately,

[1] It has been held that they did not eat with them till after Paul's agreement with James, Peter, and John : but the probabilities seem to me against this

to those of repute,[1] the Gospel which I preach
among the Gentiles, lest haply I should run or
had run in vain [a precaution, half admitting
the practical authority of Jerusalem as capable
of blocking his work]. Well, not even Titus who
was with me and a Gentile, was compelled to
be circumcised ; but [the pressure for this arose]
by reason of false brethren smuggled in, who
crept in to investigate our liberty which we have
in Christ Jesus, in order to enslave us. To them
we did not yield out of obedience even for an
hour, [and we took this stand] in order that the
truth of the Gospel might remain unto you. But
as for the leaders of repute (—their worth is a
matter of indifference to me : God is not a re-
garder of persons), well, they laid no additional
burden upon me. On the contrary, they saw
that I had been entrusted with the Gospel of
uncircumcision just as Peter had been with that
of circumcision (for He who worked for Peter
unto the apostolate of circumcision worked for
me in my turn unto the Gentiles), and they recognized the grace given to me ; and by ' they ' I
mean James and Cephas [2] and John, who were
thought to be pillars. They gave their hands
as partners to Barnabas and me, that we might

[1] The text may imply a public and a private meeting,
or just a private meeting : if the first is true, nevertheless
the private meeting was what counted.

[2] i.e. Peter.

work among the Gentiles and they among the Circumcision, provided only that we should remember the poor [i.e. of the church of Jerusalem —in effect that church as a whole], and this very thing I have been zealous to do.

' But when Cephas [1] came to Antioch, I resisted him to his face, because he was clearly in the wrong. For before some people came from James, he used to eat together with the Gentiles ; but, when they came, he drew back and separated himself, fearing the circumcised ; and the same dissembling attitude was taken also by the other Jews, so that Barnabas too was swept along with their dissimulation. But when I saw that they were not pursuing a straight course in relation to the truth of the Gospel, I said to Cephas before all, If you, being a Jew, live as the Gentiles and not as the Jews, how can you constrain the Gentiles to act as Jews ? ' The address to Peter then passes into the general discourse to the Galatians (p. 161).

This is an *ex parte* statement, made under circumstances in which any serious provable misstatement of fact would have prejudiced Paul's case, but also written with a passion which exceeds even Paul's normal tumultuous style in controversy. Serious uncertainty surrounds the reference to Titus and circumcision. An important family of MSS. and versions, commonly called

[1] i.e. Peter.

the 'Western Text', reads, 'We yielded for a season in obedience,' and makes Paul say in effect, 'Titus was not compelled to be circumcised : but as a diplomatic gesture I made a voluntary concession of the point.' The same sense, that Paul made a concession, can be found in the other reading, if the emphasis is held to fall on *obedience* : 'We yielded, but not as a matter of obedience.' The concession may sound improbable ; it has been thought possible, for firstly Paul, in spite of all the fixity and passions of his beliefs, tried to be diplomatic ; and secondly, it appears from 2 Cor. x. 10 that he was not at his most effective in face-to-face controversy. But would he have yielded on this ? The situation was not like that of Timothy, whom Paul himself circumcised (Acts xvi. 3) ; for Timothy was the son of a Jewish mother, and on Rabbinic theory obliged to be circumcised, and Paul emphatically held that except in matters of table-fellowship, in which Christian unity and charity imposed an obligation of an altogether different order, a convert should abide by the status which was his by birth, and says (1 Cor. vii. 18) : 'Is there one who was circumcised when he was called ? Let him not mend it. Is there one who was called in uncircumcision ? Let him not be circumcised.' So he might fairly hold that Timothy was by birth in the category of circumcision. But Titus ?—On the other hand, the way in which

Titus is here mentioned makes it perfectly clear that there was something to do with him out of which Paul's enemies were making capital. I venture to suggest that Paul firmly refused to circumcise Titus, or to recommend him to be circumcised, but that ' because of the false brethren ' —after mentioning whom Paul breaks off into effective but perplexing silence—Titus, under pressure, but on his own initiative and without consulting Paul, had himself circumcised in the hope of easing a difficult situation. If so, Paul is telling the truth ; and yet his enemies could plausibly maintain that in fact Paul yielded about the Gentile Titus, and so the Gentile Christians in Galatia, if they want to be other than second-best Christians, had better be circumcised themselves. The whole tenor of Paul's phrasing here suggests that he was in particular difficulty over the Titus incident.

One further inference from the passage is of special importance for what follows. It is clear that Paul and Barnabas won a first and complete victory ; a sphere of activity and a free hand in it were granted. The only obligation which Paul and Barnabas accepted was that of collecting on behalf of the Christians of Jerusalem. This would seem quite fair to them— particularly since, as practising Jews, they had learned to ascribe enormous importance to charity and almsgiving and since the Jews of the Dis-

persion regularly contributed to the Temple.
James, Peter, and John accepted the Gentile
Christian charter of liberty; if any further rati-
fication by the rest of the Twelve (if still present) was necessary, it would be purely formal.
Then trouble-makers came from Jerusalem to
Antioch; and not only Peter but Barnabas desert
Paul. The question of table-fellowship had probably not been raised in an explicit form, but Paul
could not but regard its permission as implicit
in the general approval of his ' gospel '. The
Gentile Christians were free : Jewish Christians
in a mixed community must waive their scruples
and risk eating what were according to Leviticus
xi. unclean foods. Peter was at first prepared to
accept this; but James and those who thought
as he did regarded it as no part of the agreement.
Paul criticizes Peter with extreme frankness; and
presumably without effect. Had Peter conceded
the justice of Paul's position, Paul must have
said so; it would be a trump card in his hand.[1]
There was probably no reconciliation with Peter,
and none with Barnabas. Both had seemed friends
and allies, neither being of the extreme Jewish
wing. Now there was division of the type which
provokes mutual bitterness. ' Can two walk to-

[1] The alternative hypothesis is that Paul tells the story
only to show his independence of Peter and the other
Jerusalem leaders; but the sequel does not seem to me
to fit this.

gether, except they be agreed?' In 1 Cor. ix. 6 Paul, when asserting that he has the same rights as the Apostles of Jerusalem, says, 'Or are Barnabas and I alone in not having the right not to work [but to be supported by the alms of the faithful]?' This may be thought to imply a reconciliation, but need be no more than a coupling of himself with the other great early missionary to the Gentiles. In any case, there was no reconciliation with the main body of Jewish Christians at Jerusalem.[1] Hereafter their envoys or inspectors follow at times in Paul's track, and seek to correct what are from their standpoint errors in his teaching. According to a tradition which there is no reason to doubt, Peter himself went to Corinth (p. 173).

Acts gives a different story. According to its narrative, Paul's second visit as a Christian to Jerusalem [2] (xi. 27–30) was made with Barnabas for the purpose of taking offerings from the church of Antioch to the brethren dwelling in Judaea; these offerings had been collected in consequence of the prophecy of Agabus, one of a group of prophets who had come to Antioch from Jerusalem, that there would be a great famine throughout the whole world, which happened under Claudius. There is evidence for such a famine,

[1] Mark is later a companion but not a fellow-preacher (Col. iv. 10).

[2] For the first, cf. p. 83, above.

and A.D. 46 seems a likely date. Then (Acts
xii. 25) Barnabas and Paul returned with John
Mark, whom they were to take on their missionary journey. Next (xv. 1 ff.), after the
end of that journey, certain men came down
and taught the brethren that they could not be
saved unless they were circumcised after the
custom of Moses. Paul and Barnabas argued
with them, and together with other representatives of the Antiochene church were sent to the
'Apostles and presbyteroi' in Jerusalem. After
a leisurely progress, on which they told the
brethren in Phoenicia and Samaria about the
conversion of the Gentiles, they reached Jerusalem and were received by the whole community. Here again they recounted all that God
had done by their hands, and some converted
Pharisees arose and said that their converts must
be circumcised and told to keep the Law of Moses.

The 'Apostles and presbyteroi' met; there
was much discussion, and Peter made a conciliatory speech, urging that God had made no difference between Jewish and Gentile Christians since
He had by faith cleansed the hearts of the latter,
and asking, 'Why do ye tempt God, by putting
on the neck of the disciples a yoke which neither
our fathers nor we could bear? Rather do we
believe that we are saved by the grace of the
Lord Jesus even as they.' There was silence
and Barnabas and Paul narrated the signs and

wonders which God had done among the Gentiles by their hands. Then James arose and proposed that the Gentiles should be obliged only to abstain from the pollutions of idols and from fornication and from things strangled and from blood. Accordingly, a resolution was sent by the Apostles and presbyters to the Gentile brethren in Antioch, Syria, and Cilicia, of which the tenor was : 'It seemed good to the Holy Spirit and to us to lay no burden on you over and above these necessary things, that you should abstain from meats offered to idols and from blood and from things strangled and from fornication.' This message was received with joy in Antioch, and Paul and Barnabas stayed there for a time, teaching and preaching the Gospel, till Paul proposed to Barnabas that they should make another journey ; then Barnabas wished to take John Mark again, but the memory of Mark's departure from Pamphylia caused Paul to refuse ; and their ways parted.

This narrative raises very grave difficulties. Perhaps the least is the wording of the actual decree. The 'Western Text' (p. 107, above) omits 'things strangled' and adds at the end the so-called Golden Rule, And whatsoever things you would not have done unto yourselves, do not do them to another.' The second divergent seems inappropriate, before the formal conclusion, 'Abstaining from which things you will fare well ': the first is possible, since ' things strangled ' might be an addition, intended to explain the meaning of ' blood ', which is almost certainly ' meat with blood in it ', forbidden to Jews in antiquity as to-day, and supposedly forbidden to all mankind by the ' Noachite commands ' which were thought to be divinely binding on non-Jews. Some critics have thought that ' blood ' means murder and quoted passages from Hellenistic Jewish literature in which the heathen are exhorted to abstain from idolatry, murder and fornication, as also the Rabbinic decision made during the Hadrianic persecution, that to save his life, a Jew might break all other prohibitions of the Law save these. At the same time, that is not a likely interpretation. The Gentile Christians would not naturally abstain from meat coming from a sacrifice and sold in the market, or from meat which had been killed without the blood being drained : and they needed to be told to abstain from fornication, since their earlier lives might dispose them to regard it as a matter of indifference ; but it would be strange in the same breath to bid them abstain from murder, which was as offensive to the Gentile conscience as to the Jewish. The prohibition on meat with life in it would remove one of the gravest scruples of the Jewish Christians against table-fellowship.

Coming to graver matters, we cannot reconcile

the narrative of Acts either with Galatians or with other Pauline Epistles. If Paul attended this Council, and helped to carry its decisions to Antioch, why does not he quote it as clear evidence that circumcision was not required? From his standpoint the wording was unsatisfactory, for it implied that obedience to the Decrees was a necessary minimum of the Law: in fact, an easy option. Still, if he had accepted that as a matter of policy or from that spirit of charity which he prized so highly in the relations of different groups at Corinth and at Rome (pp. 173, 217, later), would he not have quoted the Decrees against those who claimed that more of the Law, or in fact the whole Law, was obligatory? Again, why does he not refer to the Decree in his lengthy discussion in 1 Corinthians of ' meats offered to idols ', or in the discussion of food questions in Romans? Further, how are the three visits to Jerusalem in Acts to be reconciled with the two in Galatians? If we believe that the churches of Galatia are the churches in the southern part of the Roman province of that name which he founded on the first missionary journey, we can date Galatians before the Council. That view of the identity of the churches is not here accepted (p. 119): although in fairness to the reader it should be stated that many excellent scholars have held it. On their view we cannot really make the story fit Acts xi., where Paul and Barnabas are said to go up to bring relief to the church at Jerusalem. If there was a question of Titus' circumcision then, we must duplicate the controversy reported in Acts xv. Furthermore, the tone of Galatians surely implies a real interval since Paul's mission among them.

The key to the problem lies in the recognition (which has steadily gained ground) that Paul's two visits to Jerusalem, as recorded in Acts xi. and xv., are *one*, and that the author of Acts had accounts from two sources, one connecting the visit with charity, one with controversy.[1] Acts xv. is extremely tendencious. James, the spearhead of opposition, proposes the compromise ; and Peter is extremely Pauline. We are driven to accept the suggestion that the ' Decrees ' are something formulated at Jerusalem *after* Paul had secured complete recognition for the freedom of Gentile Christians,[2] and that the mention of Barnabas and Paul in them is due to redaction.[3] The ' Decrees ' were carefully disseminated and obtained a considerable currency which lasted,

[1] It seems doubtful whether we can date the visit from the famine of 46, if that be the date.

[2] Acts xxi. 25 seems to confirm this. Harnack thinks the ' Decrees ' not much earlier than the events there narrated : Lietzmann's view that they followed soon on the agreement with Paul seems more probable.

[3] So is, naturally, Acts xvi. 4, the statement that Paul and Silas gave the Apostolic Decrees to the communities which they visited in southern Asia Minor.

as we see from Rev. ii. 20-4 and later sources :
but Paul regarded them as made in bad faith
and did not feel bound by them, just as the extreme Judaizers in their turn did not stop at this
point, but sought in season and out of season
to impose the rite of circumcision and the observance of the entire Law.

CHAPTER V

PAUL'S LATER CHRISTIAN PERIOD

JERUSALEM could not be Paul's centre, and even to Antioch he only paid one more recorded visit. He had now no abiding home, and he must seek clear ground for his work, and so he set forth again with Silas (also called Silvanus), a man from the Jerusalem church. Henceforth Paul always travels with subordinates, who go to and fro, visiting the communities, and bear reports and carry letters : some are with him for long periods. One of these is the faithful Timothy, who became as a son to him (Phil. ii. 22) ; another is the man whose diary has been incorporated in Acts and constitutes the sections in which the first person plural is used (the so-called ' We sections ') ; others, from one church or another, joined him for shorter parts of his way. So he keeps contacts, under the daily burden of ' the care of all the churches ' (2 Cor. xi. 28) : in effect he must control his own organization, both to continue and supervise what he has begun, and to defeat those who seek to undo it. The only bond between him and Jerusalem now is his collection of money for the benefit of the community there : he had promised that, and he would keep his part of the bargain even when it

involved him in misunderstandings with his new
converts. The collection figures in all his epistles
from 1 Corinthians onwards to the time of his
imprisonment.

Paul's first duty was clearly to revisit and
strengthen the communities already founded in
Lystra and Derbe : then with Silas and Timothy,
whom he had pressed into service at Lystra, he went
forward. At Troas they were joined by the author
of the ' We sections ' : their route to Troas is
described with enigmatic brevity (xvi. 5). They
went through the Phrygian and Galatian territory
(*or* ' Phrygia and Galatian territory '), being prevented by the Holy Spirit from speaking the word
in Asia ; and when they came opposite Mysia they
sought to journey into Bithynia, and the Spirit of
Jesus did not allow them : so they skirted Mysia
and came to Troas. Acts refers to the first region
again in xviii. 23, where Paul on his way to Ephesus
' goes through in order the Galatian territory and
Phrygia, strengthening all the disciples '.

This ' Galatian territory ' and the ' Galatians ' to
whom Paul addressed an important Epistle have
commonly been referred to the region of Asia
Minor in which invading Celts settled in the third
century B.C. This view involves difficulties, and
Sir William Ramsay has argued with great skill
and learning that the reference to Galatia and
Galatians is to be interpreted in terms of the large
Roman province of Galatia, which included the

region of Lycaonia : here Acts would be speaking of the ' Phrygian region of Galatia ', and Paul's Epistle would be addressed not to its inhabitants but to churches in the southern part of the province, and in fact to the churches of Lystra, Derbe and Iconium which he and Barnabas had founded on the first missionary journey and which he revisited on the second. The balance of probability seems to me to be against this theory, but the reader should bear it in mind and remember that the letter may be addressed to the ' South Galatians ' even if the references in Acts xvi. 6 and xviii. 23 are not to them.

These interventions of the Spirit to direct or inhibit Paul's movements may seem to us an artificial literary device : but the Epistles show clearly that he did in fact believe himself to receive direct divine guidance—for instance, the inspiration to go with Barnabas to Jerusalem (p. 105), and so the device, if it is a device, is appropriate.[1] The climax follows at Troas : ' a vision appeared to Paul in the night : there was a Macedonian standing and exhorting him and saying, Come over to Macedonia and help us ' (xvi. 9). This departure needed special explanation in the narrative. Paul had plenty of work to do in Asia Minor ; events showed that it was a particularly favourable soil for Christian missionary enterprise, partly perhaps because of some laxity of Judaism. We

[1] Cf. p. 136, later.

cannot build on a Talmudic saying which has been translated as 'the wine of Phrygia and its baths have separated the Ten Tribes from their brethren';[1] but the Revelation, which is thoroughly Jewish in sentiment, speaks (ii. 9) of the reviling which the church of Smyrna received 'from those who say that they are Jews and are not, but are the synagogue of Satan'. Their opposition to Christianity is plain : but so also is the fact that among such Jews, who had lost their traditional piety and adjustment to life, there would be many who would be dissatisfied with themselves and easily receptive of new convictions.

Paul was taken to Macedon by a strong impulse, like the romantic impulses which are recorded in the life of Alexander the Great. The world was Paul's parish : and it may well be that his thoughts were already turning to Rome. He founded churches in Philippi, Thessalonica, and Beroea. In each he encountered serious opposition, and the form which it took at Philippi was significant as a foretaste of much later antipathy to Christianity. The owners of a slave-girl who was thought to be possessed and who uttered prophecies which were a source of gain to them until Paul exorcized her, brought Paul and Silas before the magistrates and said, ' These men, being Jews, greatly disturb our city and preach customs which we, being

[1] A. Neubauer, *Géographie du Talmud*, p. 315; but see I. Lévy, *Revue des Etudes juives*, XLI (1900), p. 183 ff.

Romans, are not permitted to accept or follow' (xvi. 20 f.). Philippi was a Roman colony, and the mob supported the accusers, and Paul and Silas were scourged and thrown into prison : probably Paul had not time to claim the immunity from stripes which as a Roman citizen he possessed, or else his plea was disregarded in the excitement of the moment, as such pleas often were. The statement of the accusers was unsound in strict law, but sound in sentiment : that is to say, a Roman citizen as such had no legal obligation to worship the gods of Rome and was not normally prohibited from attaching himself to other cults, but patriotism found something repellent in the other loyalties of the proselyte or the Christian.[1]

At Thessalonica, where Paul received financial aid from the Philippians (Phil. iv. 16), another charge, also destined for a long life, was levelled against Paul and Silas. 'These men who have upset the world are here too, and Jason has received them into his house : and all of them are acting contrary to Caesar's edicts, saying there is another king, Jesus' (xvii. 6-7). In the last analysis, Pilate's approval of the death-sentence on Jesus turned precisely on this. The inscription on the Cross, 'The king of the Jews', tells its tale and was no doubt meant to discourage any other would-be kings. The Roman state was just and tolerant :

[1] Paul perhaps left the author of the ' We sections ' at Philippi to supervise the community.

it never interfered in religious matters save when public order seemed to be threatened ; but it would not and could not tolerate any rival sovereignty. The Christian expectation of a new kingdom was very liable to be misunderstood.

The Macedonian mission bore good fruit, but the opposition to Paul compelled him to move on, and he went to Athens. Here he talked in the synagogue to the Jews and to those Gentiles who frequented Jewish worship, and in the marketplace to any whom he encountered. What would we not give for a record of one of those conversations, and how far did Paul succeed in becoming, as he claims to have done, ' a Greek to the Greeks ' ? No opposition in the synagogue is reported here : it was probably a small body, but the likeliest explanation is that the writer of Acts, who has not a little conscious artistry, wanted to vary his usual style of relating the history of a Pauline mission, and to focus attention on his skilful scene of Paul before the court of Areopagus.

In any case, Paul's experience at Athens must have been different from his experience at the cities which he had previously visited, for Athens was a different place. It had been the most powerful of Greek cities during the fifth century before Christ : then it was a world-power, and apart from Persia the greatest world-power of the age. At the same time, it was the literary and artistic centre of the Greek world. Its political predominance was broken by the disastrous end of the Peloponnesian war in 404, but it speedily regained considerable power, and continued to be the undisputed leader in culture. After Philip of Macedon's decisive victory at Chaeronea in 338, and the introduction of the Hellenistic era of monarchies, its power was reduced, but not brought to nothing. New cultural centres came into being ; Alexandria and Pergamon in particular were fostered as part of the façade of the Ptolemaic and Attalid dynasties ; but Athens had a primacy of tradition, and in philosophy she was still the most important city. Then came the disaster. Rome's policy in the Near East in the second century was marked by a somewhat clumsy stupidity and provoked increasing resentment. In 88 B.C. Mithridates, the king of Pontus, declared what was practically a holy war on Rome ; and the Greek cities of the province of Asia (the Western end of Asia Minor) rallied to his support and massacred the Romans resident in them. Athens also joined him and was captured after a long siege by the Roman general Cornelius Sulla. The war and the peace ruined her for good and all. She became in effect a university city, to which came those who wished to make a serious study of philosophy and also sons of distinguished Romans who wished to learn as much of it as would be good for them, in the company of the sons of other distinguished Romans. Otherwise there were the mysteries of Eleusis, to which even emperors came to be initiated, and the temples and the works of art and memories and bitter poverty.

One thing had not changed : the liking for good talk. As Acts xvii. 21 says : ' Now all the Athenians and the strangers in the city had time for nothing save to say something or to hear something new.' Paul was sure to command interest as a novel phenomenon. He was doubtless thought to be some kind of itinerant lecturer on philosophy, and as such was brought before the court of Areopagus, a distinguished body so called as having originally met on the small mound called the Hill of Ares. At this time it in effect governed the city and, while not licensing lecturers, took some cognizance of them. We know that Cicero commended to this body the Peripatetic philosopher Cratippus, who wished to lecture at Athens.[1]

Those who brought Paul before the Areopagus are reported to have said (xvii. 19) : ' Can we know what is this new teaching which you are spreading ? You bring to our ears some things which have a strange ring : so we wish to know what they mean.' Accordingly he came to give an account of himself. The speech reported is a brilliant piece of imaginative writing.

There is no reason to suppose that this is a report of what Paul said. First, the habit of Greek

[1] It is possible that the whole setting is invented, to make a scene of contrast.

and Roman historians was to put speeches of their own composition into the mouths of their characters. To have reproduced the actual words, even if they were available, would have seemed bad style, as destroying the unity of expression of a work. Nearly all the characters in Acts talk in one style.[1] Secondly, in all probability there was no such thing at Athens as an altar dedicated *To an unknown God*. Paul might have seen *either* an altar with no inscription, *or* an altar inscribed ' To unknown gods '—set up by someone who thought a given spot uncanny and numinous, and did not know the name of the deity to whom he ought to pay homage : but it is extremely unlikely that Paul can have seen an altar with this inscription. Thirdly, the speech is the pendant of the short utterance at Lystra (p. 93, above) : both are the writer's idea of how Paul would have addressed a Gentile audience.

At the same time, some of the speeches in Acts appear to rest on earlier documents and it is very likely that Paul did speak somewhat as he is represented : that is to say, that he would start with ground common to himself and part at least of his audience. In addressing Jews he would start with the Old Testament and God's Plan for Israel,

---

[1] There is matter of a probably historical kind in Stephen's speech (p. 62) : probably there was some special memory of the line Stephen took, which had descended to a source used in Acts.

and gradually introduce Christian interpretation of prophetic passages, and end on an exhortation to repent quickly while there was time. Here he starts from a Stoic view of God, as creator and benefactor and immanent; introduces the notion of men's search for God, who is nevertheless not far from each one of us; attacks idolatry, as many philosophers did; and then comes to the exhortation to repentance.

The idea of repentance was not wholly unfamiliar to Gentile circles: but when Paul proceeds to give as a reason the impending Judgment, by the man appointed by God and guaranteed to all as such by being raised from the dead, ' some mocked, and others said: We will hear you on this topic another time also '. As for Judgment, the audience would be familiar with the notion of each individual being judged as an individual after death, and being assigned reward or punishment according to his merits. But the notion that the resurrection of Jesus guaranteed him as a destined judge sounded merely silly, and if Paul talked of the resurrection of the body in a general way, he would get a very unsympathetic hearing. The Epicureans indeed supposed the soul to be material, like the body, and destined to be resolved into its elements when the body died: most other thinkers deemed it to be wholly different from the body and many held it to be divine and immortal, now prisoned in the body but destined if virtuous to be released

at death : but the body's fate seemed obviously
' ashes to ashes, dust to dust ', and many thought
it a good riddance.

Paul is reported to have made some converts,
including Dionysius, a member of the court of
Areopagus and therefore a person of substance,
and a woman called Damaris, whose presence in
the crowd has suggested that she was of very different status. But the mission cannot have been
very successful, and Paul moved on to Corinth,
where, as at Antioch, conditions were eminently
favourable for his work. It is easier to convert
the Prodigal Son than his brother or his uncle
who is a professor. The ancient city of Corinth
had grown to great commercial activity and wealth,
thanks to its position on the isthmus. It had been
a place of luxury and lax ways, and the fame of
its courtesans was not ended when its material
prosperity declined in the fourth century B.C.
In 146 B.C. it rose against Rome and suffered a
destruction, which archaeologists have shown to
have been less complete than ancient writers suggest. The site was abandoned for a century, till
in 46 B.C. a Roman colony was founded there, and
prospered. The cults were continued, as that of
Aphrodite and the worship of Egyptian Isis and
Sarapis.

At Corinth Paul had the luck to make new
friends—a Jew called Aquila, born in Pontus, and
his wife Priscilla (also called Prisca). Several times

in the New Testament Priscilla is mentioned before Aquila, and this is so unusual as to have provoked the conjecture that she was of higher station— perhaps a woman of civic birth who had become a proselyte and married a Jewish freedman. They had left Rome in consequence of an edict of Claudius banishing Jews from the city. The late historian Orosius dates this in 49, which is probably right within a year. Aquila was, like Paul, a tent-maker, and they worked together: they were to meet again at Ephesus.

Paul was at first well received in the synagogue, but had to leave and dwell in the house of Titus Justus, who 'worshipped God'—that is to say, probably a Gentile who had leanings towards Judaism (p. 26, above). The house was next door to the synagogue, which hardly made for better feelings, particularly when Crispus, a leading official of the Jewish community, became a Christian. Paul taught here for a year and a half, with great success. From here he wrote the two letters to the Thessalonians (p. 147). Timothy had brought a report of conditions there, which indicated that the attacks made on Paul had continued to be directed against the community, and that they had manfully resisted persecution: at the same time, they were somewhat troubled about certain questions, in particular questions relating to the expected Coming of Christ, and Paul, who was anxious and strained (1 Cor ii. 3), felt, in fact, obliged to send a second letter, very much in the same vein as the first, to correct a misunderstanding which his first letter might be in danger of creating or encouraging (pp. 154–6, later).

Towards the end of Paul's stay, the Jews brought him before the proconsul Gallio, charging that he sought to persuade men to worship God in an illegal manner ; but Gallio dismissed the charge in a few contemptuous words. The incident, which has given a proverb to the English language ('But Gallio cared for none of these things '), affords to the historian a chronological indication more dependable than the expulsion of the Jews from Rome (p. 207) : for an inscription at Delphi dates Gallio's proconsulship in A.D. 51–2 (possibly 52–3).[1] Paul stayed on for a fair number of days —so says Acts, emphasizing that he took no harm when accused before a Roman proconsul and not before some local tribunal which could be swayed by prejudice, mob violence, or ill-founded charges. Then he set out for Syria, putting in at Ephesus. Here he left Aquila and Priscilla, stopping himself only long enough to preach in the synagogue : when pressed to stay he replied that, God willing,

---

[1] The dates for later events in Paul's life depend on the statements in Acts about the lengths of his various stays. If the end of Felix's procuratorship (p. 140, later) could be dated in 55, we should have a fixed point : but that is far from certain and perhaps does not allow enough margin of time.

he would return. Clearly he wished to make trial of the ground at Ephesus, having guessed rightly that it was likely to be as good a field for work as Corinth had proved. It could be more : it was a centre at which Paul could keep in touch with his new churches in Macedonia, with his older churches in South-east Asia Minor, and with Antioch. From this centre Paul was to organize his collection for the benefit of the church at Jerusalem (p. 111, above). From Ephesus he sailed to Caesarea, and went up and saluted ' the church '—which in all probability means ' the church of Jerusalem ' : thence he proceeded to Antioch and stayed for a time, presumably to rest, if indeed he could rest.

In the meanwhile Aquila and Priscilla had made an important contribution (xviii. 24) : ' Now a Jew called Apollos, an Alexandrian by birth, a man of culture (or, an eloquent man : *logios* is vague), came to Ephesus, being powerful in the scriptures. He had been instructed in the way of the Lord, and being fervent with the Spirit spoke and taught accurately the things concerning Jesus, although he knew only the baptism of John ; and he began to speak freely in the synagogue. Priscilla and Aquila heard him, and laid hold on him and taught him the Way of God more accurately.' Apollos has sometimes been regarded as a disciple of John the Baptist ; if so, he could know ' the things concerning Jesus ' only in so far as

John explained Messianic prophecy, though in that case the phrase would ideally be ' the things concerning the Christ '. In any case, he knew also ' the Way of the Lord ' : and probably he was a man who had heard or learned of the actual teaching of Jesus in the flesh, but had not learned the teaching developed at Jerusalem and elsewhere about Jesus as the Risen Lord, and about the Spirit as a gift regularly bestowed by God upon the baptized. Apollos, after this instruction, wished to go to Achaea : and the brethren wrote to the disciples to receive him, which is the first recorded instance of a practice, later important, whereby a Christian going from one community to another received letters of commendation (cf. 2 Cor. iii. 1). Apollos was well received at Corinth, where his scriptural learning made him an effective missioner to the Jews. At the same time, his coming was no unmixed blessing, for the disciples and initiates of the various Christian teachers developed a considerable intensity of party feeling, which we must discuss later (p. 173).

Meanwhile, Paul set out on another journey, beginning with a tour of ' the Galatian country and Phrygia ' (p. 119, above), where he strengthened the disciples, and then arriving at Ephesus. An energetic mission followed—for three months in the synagogue, for two years in the hall of Tyrannus ; and Ephesus became a centre from which Christian teaching radiated through the province of Asia, and Paul's disciples founded the communities of Colossae (where Epaphras taught), Laodicea (where Archippus taught), and Hierapolis. The work at Ephesus was a great success, but it provoked bitter conflict (1 Cor. xvi. 8–9). In 1 Cor. xv. 32, the second of the letters which Paul wrote from Ephesus to Corinth (p. 172, below), Paul speaks of 'having fought with beasts in Ephesus': this must be a metaphor, since he could not have been condemned to the arena without losing the Roman citizenship to which he appealed in Jerusalem and Caesarea, but implies a dispute of more than ordinary intensity. Finally he had to leave Ephesus after a riot in the theatre, arising out of a charge that Paul had led astray great numbers, not only in Ephesus but in almost all Asia, and that he threatened the fame and popularity of the temple of the great goddess Artemis. Artemis of Ephesus was a pre-Greek deity bearing a Greek name, but retaining many native elements in her worship and having as her most sacred idol a meteorite. She was the leading deity of the city and was worshipped far and wide as Ephesian Artemis. General criticism of pagan myth and cult was one thing : philosophers had done plenty of that and nearly always with impunity. But anything that seemed to touch the prestige of Artemis of the Ephesians at Ephesus itself was another thing and a very dangerous thing : the mob cried for two hours in the theatre, ' Great

is Artemis of the Ephesians ', and if they had got
their hands on Paul his Roman citizenship would
not have interested them. His life was saved,
but he was in grave peril, and what happened
was a grievous affliction. Paul had built at Ephesus
the most important Christian structure which it
was given to him to raise—a community of great
life and vigour, from which Christianity radiated
abroad. In modern parlance he had founded a
diocese and not a congregation.

So he left, and made a tour of inspection in
Macedonia and Greece, returning through Macedonia. It was a troublous time, in which the
well-being of the Corinthian church gave him
much anxiety ; he had already been compelled to
make a flying visit to meet an emergency (pp. 172,
202, below). One of the letters which he sent to
them reminds us of the amount of his experience
which we do not know from Acts (2 Cor. xi.
23 ff.) : ' Are they servants of Christ ? I speak
as a madman, but I am so in a supreme degree ;
in labours more abundantly, in imprisonments
more abundantly, in stripes surpassingly, in fears
of death ' (*literally* ' in deaths ') ' often. From the
Jews I have five times received forty stripes save
one. Thrice was I beaten with rods, once was I
stoned, thrice shipwrecked : a night and a day
have I spent in the deep ; in journeys often, in
perils by rivers, in perils by robbers, in perils
from my own race, in perils from Gentiles, in perils

in cities, in perils in the open country, in perils on the sea, in perils among false brethren, in labour and toil, in sleeplessness often, in hunger and thirst, in fastings often, in cold and nakedness.' If we compare this test with the narrative in Acts up to date, we can identify one imprisonment and one beating with rods (at Philippi), the one stoning (at Lystra), and some perils from Jews and from Gentiles : all the rest belongs to stories that were not recorded.

From Philippi he sailed to Troas, where a delegation from the Macedonian communities [1] and three men from Asia awaited him ; the Macedonians probably bore the contributions of their churches to Paul's collection of money for the church of Jerusalem. He then continued a coasting voyage, having determined not to stop at Ephesus, lest he should spend time in Asia : his purpose was to be at Jerusalem for the Jewish feast of Pentecost, which was celebrated seven weeks after the Passover. Nevertheless, he summoned the *presbyteroi* of the Ephesian church to meet him at Miletus and addressed them : the speech reported in Acts xx. 18–35, while it must be ascribed to the writer of the book and not to Paul, is a singularly moving and appropriate composition. He has taught all, Jews and Gentiles alike, ' repentance before God

---

[1] For *Gaius of Derbe* in the R.V. (xx. 4) probably read *Gaius of Doberus* (a Macedonian city), a reading divined by A. C. Clark from the ' Western text '.

and faith in our Lord Jesus '. ' And now, behold, bound in the Spirit I go to Jerusalem, not knowing what will happen to me there, save that the Holy Spirit testifies to me in every city, saying that chains and afflictions await me.' No abnormal powers of discernment were needed—either in Paul or in the ' prophets ' of communities—to inform him that a visit to Jerusalem was a very dangerous enterprise. Rom. xv. 31 (p. 219, later) illustrates this perfectly. The Jewish Christians suspected and often opposed him ; and to other Jews he was, as he has remained in Jewish tradition, anathema. The annual visits of men from the Dispersion to Jerusalem would carry plenty of news of his activities—notably at Ephesus. When Paul arrived at Jerusalem, James is represented as saying to him (xxi. 20 f.), ' Do you see, brother, what multitudes there are among the Jews of men who have believed (in Christ), and they are all fanatics for the Law ? Now they have been informed concerning you that you teach all Jews living among the Gentiles to apostatize from Moses, telling them not to circumcise their children nor to walk according to the customs.' We may well be somewhat sceptical about this reference to the multitude (*literally*, ' myriads ') of Jewish Christians : the danger was from ordinary Jews, though many Jewish Christians would be at best lukewarm in Paul's support, and perhaps willing to sacrifice him in the. interests of better relations with their

fellow Jews in general. Some of the latter probably felt that Paul's activities meant ruin to the
proselytizing activity of Jews. The Gentiles would
not embrace the Law of Moses when they were
offered this easier way to the Life of the World
to Come ; so it would be said, and the opposition
could be intensified by some of the more extreme
utterances which controversy had wrung from him.

Paul is then made to say that he reckons his
life as nothing in comparison with accomplishing
his course and the ministry which he has received
from Jesus of testifying to the Gospel of the grace
of God. He proceeds to exhort the presbyters to
pastoral care and entrusts them to Christ. His
journey continues to Caesarea and thence to Jerusalem. Here James gives him the warning just
quoted, and advises him to make a politic gesture
of loyalty to Judaism, namely, to pay the expenses
of the vow of four Jewish Christians and share
their fast. This he did,[1] but towards the end of
the period, some Jews from Asia, who doubtless
knew of the success of Paul's mission at Ephesus,
saw him in the Temple and laid hands on him,
charging him with having defiled the Temple

---

[1] This has been disputed, as inconsistent with Paul's
general attitude towards the Law : but would he not
have regarded it as a conciliatory act of *agape* (p. 196,
later), and therefore wholly right since it did not infringe
the religious liberty of Gentile Christians ? Cf. 1 Cor.
ix. 21.

by bringing Gentiles into it. This was a most serious charge : the Roman authorities permitted the Jews to execute any Gentile found in the Inner Court.

The whole city was moved, and a mob seized Paul and dragged him out of the Temple, and would most certainly have killed him had not the commander of the Roman garrison heard of it. He acted at once, as any British Colonial administrator would be bound to do to-day : his duty was to deal with the situation while it was manageable. There had been plenty of trouble in recent years in Judaea, and this riot, if not quelled, might mean an insurrection which would require the use of the legions under the command of the governor of Syria and cost Rome both men and money. Accordingly, the commander secured Paul's person and would have scourged him to force a confession of what the trouble was, had not Paul claimed the privilege of immunity which belonged to him as a Roman citizen. On the face of it, Paul looked like one of the agitators who had been such a nuisance. That the commander, as Acts says, before thinking of the torture allowed Paul to address the people, and to produce the further infuriation which was inevitable, must appear highly doubtful : it would have been so stupid.

The commander knew that this was a case for the governor, and that a report of the circumstances attending the riot was required. It is quite credible that, as Acts relates, he ordered a meeting of the Sanhedrin and set Paul before them, for the case seemed to be a matter involving Jewish religious scruples and the Sanhedrin ought to be able to help him to get some idea of what was at stake. It is equally credible that what happened in the Sanhedrin was no more than mutual recrimination : Paul maintaining that he was a good Jew, nay rather a good Pharisee, and that there was nothing against him except that, like any other Pharisee, he believed in the resurrection, and the meeting going cheerfully after the red herring. Ananias was not a creditable high priest ; and Paul's passionate reply, ' God shall smite thee, thou whited wall,' is quite natural. But, if he did say it, it may have been remembered against him by the Roman authorities, since an insult to the Jewish high priest would be an offence against public order.

The commander left the meeting none the wiser, and, learning of a plot to assassinate Paul, removed him under strong guard to Caesarea, where he could much more easily be kept in safety. At Caesarea he was brought before the governor, Felix, who was the brother of Pallas, a man who had come to Rome as a slave, been manumitted and attained great power as a member of the private administratorship of the Emperor Claudius. Felix, whose wife was a Jewish princess, awaited

the accusers and after five days they came—
Ananias, some ' elders ', and an orator called
Tertullus whom they had retained to plead their
case. The accusation proved to be that Paul
stirred up factions among all Jews throughout the
world, and had tried to profane the Temple. This
would legally involve the crime of *maiestas*, ' high
treason ', an exceedingly elastic category : and, on
the face of it, did not lack plausibility ; whatever
Paul might say for himself, there had been riots
in many places where he had been, and the Roman
government did not like riots. Paul replied with
a statement of his innocence and of his beliefs.
Felix decided to defer a decision : he had an
unlimited legal right to do this, and it was the
easiest way to act.

' And when a two-year period was completed,
Felix received as successor Porcius Festus ; and
wishing to earn favour with the Jews he left
Paul in prison.' These words raise a very difficult chronological problem. What is the two-year
period ? that of Paul's imprisonment, or that of
the governorship of Felix ? On the whole, I think
the first.

When Festus arrived and visited Jerusalem, the
local authorities made vigorous representations that
Paul should be brought back to Jerusalem ; they
intended an ambush, for which the Palestinian
countryside is eminently suitable. Festus replied
by suggesting that competent persons should come

down to Caesarea and make any charges which they had against Paul. They did so, but the proceedings were inconclusive—assertion and counter-assertion. Festus asked Paul whether he was willing to be tried in Jerusalem. Paul refused : although the trial would be before Festus, Jerusalem involved point-less danger and also an atmosphere of prejudice : Festus might be tempted to sacrifice him to Jewish sentiment in the interests of peace, if not in his personal interests. Accordingly he appealed to Caesar : that is to say, he demanded, as his right through citizenship, that his case should be heard by the emperor's own tribunal. At Rome he would have a good chance of a fair trial. Had Festus been willing to release him, the risk of assassination was extreme ; and in any case, as we know from Romans (p. 207, later), Paul eagerly desired to go to Rome. His appeal in effect deprived Festus of competence to hear the case. When king Herod Agrippa II, who had some personal authority in connection with the Temple, came with Berenice to pay his respects to the new governor, Festus spoke of Paul to Agrippa and permitted Agrippa to hear what Paul had to say : doubtless he hoped to learn from Agrippa a little more of what was at stake, in order that he might give a fuller account to the Emperor.

Paul and other prisoners went to Rome, and after delays from bad weather and shipwreck landed at Puteoli. There were Christians here who wel-comed him : their presence is very natural in a port-town, where in like manner Semitic and Egyptian cults had early been established. He was allowed to stay seven days with them, and journeyed to Rome, being met by Christians thence : on arrival, he was allowed to live by himself with the soldier who guarded him. At Rome he is said to have summoned the leaders of the Jewish community to meet him and to have declared to them his innocence of any offence against the People or its ancestral customs : ' I wear this chain because of the hope of Israel.' They replied, saying that they had had no letters nor heard any evil reports concerning him, and would like to hear his ideas : what they knew about this ' sect ' was that it was everywhere criticized. Accordingly, they appointed a day on which he talked to them on the theme of the argument from prophecy : some hearkened, others disbelieved : and Paul quoted a prophecy to show that it was foretold that the Jews would not hear and that salvation was sent to the Gentiles. The scene, if taken literally, is impossible : it stands here for dramatic effect.

The closing sentences of Acts describe Paul as abiding for two whole years and receiving all who came to see him, ' proclaiming the Kingdom of God and teaching the things concerning Jesus Christ, in open speech, without let or hindrance '. This is a note of triumph ; as Roman prisoner Paul was after all not exposed to many of the earlier perils of his life. But what was the sequel ? The letters from captivity (Chap. IX) imply now danger, now hope. The First Epistle of Clement, written about the close of the century, speaks of Paul as having gone to the bounds of the West and testified before rulers and also states that Peter and he lost their lives as a result of envy (in such a way, moreover, as to imply that both died in Rome) : no acquittal is mentioned. The so-called Pastoral Epistles (p. 231), which are probably somewhat later, refer to a ' first defence ' and were interpreted by Eusebius, the fourth-century church historian, as implying that he was acquitted at his first trial and later arrested again and aware that death was imminent : but this interpretation may be false. In subsequent years the tradition became clearer : the Muratorian Canon, a list of the accepted books of the New Testament, compiled about the end of the second century, expressly mentions Paul's departure from Rome for Spain.

Once more we cannot know the truth : the statement that Paul went to Spain would so easily come into existence as a result of Rom. xv. 24, where such a journey is described as an old plan of Paul's. Further, the Neronian persecution of 64 was well known to the later Church and there was every temptation to make Paul's death fall within it. Accordingly, it is quite possible that Paul did not escape from his first imprisonment, either by acquittal or through the charges lapsing. There was a body of evidence likely to suggest to an Imperial functionary that Paul was a trouble-maker of a serious order; if then any external incident occurred to interest the authorities in Jewish affairs, or if Jews in Rome made interest with Poppaea, Nero's mistress and later wife, Paul could perfectly well have been condemned to death for *maiestas* (p. 140, above). In any case, he died for his faith, and the Roman Church showed an unerring instinct for underlying truth when it canonized Peter and Paul as its two founders.

CHAPTER VI

THE TRAVEL LETTERS : I. THESSALONIANS
AND GALATIANS

THE Pauline Epistles fall into two main groups :
the letters written on journeys—1 and 2 Thessalonians, 1 and 2 Corinthians, Galatians and Romans :
and the letters from prison, Colossians, Philemon,
and Philippians. Ephesians, which is probably not
genuine, and the Pastoral Epistles (1 and 2 Timothy
and Titus), which are almost certainly not, will be
handled with the second group. Hebrews is certainly neither by Paul nor Pauline, and we shall
leave it out of consideration.

In the ancient world the category of the letter
covered anything, from the briefest and most
intimate note to edicts by kings and magistrates,
formal memorials and brief monographs dedicated
to a person or group. Cicero's correspondence
covers the whole range, including as it does the
treatise on electioneering addressed by his brother
Quintus to him, and political manifestos in which
he uses the rhythms of formal oratorical prose.
Letters of this elaborate type, and some shorter
ones, were copied and sent to men other than those

to whom they were addressed. Even in our own time the Open Letter is still a form of literature.

Paul's Epistles are the beginning of a new type —the Pastoral and Encyclical letters issued by Bishops and Popes, serving to convey messages which cannot be conveyed by word of mouth. They took the place of exhortations which absence prevented him from giving at solemn meetings of his communities, reviving memories of shared experience and strengthening the bonds of affection. They include formulas of prayer and praise which take us directly into the worship of the churches ; the greeting at the end of 2 Cor. xiii. could have preceded immediately the Eucharistic celebration. Paul used this with peculiar skill, retaining all the vigour of the spoken word. In the struggles of his life this was the one weapon which he could use as no one else. His enemies appear to have gone to the length of issuing forged letters in his name, a device which he sometimes met by a salutation in his own hand following the text which he dictated (2 Thess. iii. 17 ; Col. iv. 18) ; of Galatians he wrote at least the postscript (Gal. vi. 11). How effective his Epistles were can be seen from the remark of an enemy, quoted 2 Cor. x. 10, ' For his Epistles are weighty and powerful, but his bodily presence weak and his speech contemptible.'

Let us for a moment put ourselves in the position of the group of Christians at Thessalonica who at their weekly meeting for worship, on one Sunday in 50 or 51 or at very latest early 52, heard 1 Thessalonians read, as a letter from Paul, then in Corinth, to the community.[1]   First, the greeting : ' Paul and Silvanus and Timothy '—in this letter Paul throughout associates his fellow-workers with himself : ' to the church of the Thessalonians in God the Father and the Lord Jesus Christ '—that describes the new plane of life to which the Christians have now been transported : ' grace to you and peace ' :—*charis*, grace, though referring to a specifically Christian gift, enjoyed by reception rather than by effort, might suggest the *chairein*, ' greeting ', with which Greek letters are often started, but the meaning is wholly different—' peace ' was the Jewish greeting, *shalom*, used then as now.   Next Paul gave thanks to God for the loyalty of the community—which corresponds to the prayer for the recipient or other pious phrase which often opens a popular letter of the time :   Paul starts like this, even in the brief personal note to Philemon : the form is changed in 2 Corinthians, but there is something corresponding, the significant exception is Galatians (p. 162, later).   Here he thanks God for their ' work of faith and labour of love, *agape*, and constancy of hope in our Lord Jesus Christ before our God and Father '—anticipating the famous triad of virtues in 1 Cor. xiii. (p. 197) ; there are certain

[1] Throughout this and the following chapter what is put between single inverted commas is often a loose paraphrase of Paul's argument.

personal qualities which, as in Hellenistic Judaism, bring men near to God, and one of these is *agape*, the loving mutual consideration and helpfulness which was for Paul the touchstone of Christian conduct. Each produces a fruit in life.

Paul speaks of the election of the Thessalonians : God has chosen them—that is always the basic notion of the Kingdom (p. 38, above)—and the preaching proved to be not in word only but in power and in the Holy Spirit. He says that they have imitated him and the Lord in receiving the word under affliction with the joy of the Holy Spirit, and have become a model to all the churches in Macedonia and Achaea :—this joy was for Paul a principal note of the Christian life : it is not *eudaimonia* 'happiness', or *hedone*, 'pleasure', terms absent from Paul's vocabulary. We may also remark that he shows an extreme happiness in being able to praise anything in his communities. People tell, Paul continues, of his visit to Thessalonica and of how the Thessalonians have turned from idols to serve the living and true God, and await the advent from heaven of his Son whom he raised from the dead, Jesus who rescues us from the coming wrath :— so the hearers are predominantly Gentiles, and the message which they have received is, as in Acts xiv. and xvii. (p. 101, above), one of urgency : 'the Judge is at the gate' and Jesus will be the advocate and defender of his own. This reference to the future appears in all the thanksgiving save that of Romans.

This brief paragraph sums up much Pauline teaching : salvation is from the judgment by gifts of God and the Spirit : man's function is receptivity and the attitudes which flow from it. Paul then, perhaps as a result of criticisms arising from the vehement hostility of the Macedonian Jews and reported to him, but perhaps merely in order to make his position clear to a group who knew of wandering teachers of various types, and also by way of moral exhortation, reminds the Church of his modest but outspoken attitude in preaching, and his failure to assume the airs appropriate to apostles of Christ [1] and to live at the expense of his converts. They in their turn had received it, not as a word of man—which presumably some people maintained— but, as what it really was, God's word working in those who believed. They had imitated the churches in Judaea in Christ Jesus, for they had suffered from people of their own race just as those churches had at the hands of the Jews, who killed both the Lord Jesus and the prophets. (Here we see the mood of Stephen's speech, p. 62, above ; Paul does not make such outbursts later.)

What is the meaning of this recurrent *in Christ*

---

[1] This statement (ii. 9) may be understood as covering also Silvanus and Timothy (cf. ii. 18), but in all probability it refers simply to Paul. They would all follow the same policy about money. Burkitt was inclined to credit Silvanus with some part in the putting together of this and the following letter.

Jesus ? It describes the medium in which Christian life was lived, a medium essential to it just as water is to the existence of fish : it is parallel to ' in the body ', ' in the flesh ', ' in sin ', ' in Spirit '. This is no metaphor ; it describes what Paul believed to be literal fact. In 1 Corinthians he constantly uses it, not as a figure of speech, but as a basis of arguments, as for instance in i. 13, apropos of their factions, ' Is Christ divided ? ' Consider above all vi. 15–17. Paul is arguing against fornication and says, ' Do you not know that your bodies are limbs of Christ ? Shall I then take the limbs of Christ and make them the limbs of a harlot ? Let it not be ! Or do you not know that he who cleaves to a harlot is one body with her ? *For they twain*, it is written, *shall be one flesh* (Gen. ii. 24). But he who cleaves to the Lord is one spirit (with him).' Exactly the same quasi-physical notion is implied in the argument against divorcing a non-Christian partner in marriage : 1 Cor. vii. 14, ' For the un-believing man is sanctified in his wife, and the unbelieving wife is sanctified in her husband : since otherwise your children would be impure, whereas now they are holy.' The physical union of man and woman can transfer something of the saving corporality of Christ : even when it is the woman who is the Christian (I say ' even when ' because of 1 Cor. xi. 3 ' the head of every man is Christ, the head of woman is man, the head of Christ is God '). This is a hard saying, but it is Pauline.

Such transferred holiness is not salvation—it is only the possibility of salvation : even those fully in Christ could lapse. Paul reverts to the idea in xii. 27, ' You are the body of Christ and his several limbs.' Did not the Spirit of Christ fill and animate the believers as it filled and animated the glorified transformation of his earthly body ? As men live ' in Christ ', so they fall asleep ' in Christ ' and will be brought to fresh life ' in Christ ' (xv. 22). In this last passage we have the antithesis of Adam, whose fall was regarded as standing in a close connection with the presence and power of sin and death. As all died in Adam, so all will be brought to life in Christ—by dying and rising again with him in baptism (p. 214, later).[1] All humanity was believed to be in Adam (quite literally, to come of his seed) ; all Christian humanity was in Christ. The first Adam was a living soul, *psyche* : the last Adam, a life-giving spirit (xv. 45) : hence the difference of ' in Christ ' and ' in Adam '. A quasi-physical change takes place in the believer : he must realize its consequences. When the believer is ' in Christ ', he belongs to a new solidarity, in which the merits of one member can help another (2 Cor. viii. 14 ; Col. i. 24), and the mind (i.e. spirit) of the Christians is the mind (i.e. spirit) of Christ (1 Cor. ii. 16).

Reverting to 1 Thess. ii. 14, Paul speaks in a very

---

[1] Baptism ' into the name of Jesus Christ ' may imply the same idea : but the phrase need not mean more than that the act is performed in relation to Jesus Christ.

appreciative way of the churches in Judaea : presumably if the ' Decrees ' had been passed (p. 113, above), there was as yet no active opposition of the type described in Galatians. The slaying of ' Jesus and the prophets ' shows that Paul, like Stephen, regarded the death of Jesus as the climax of a long series of kindred incidents : Jesus had spoken of Jerusalem as killing the prophets (Matt. xxiii. 37).

Paul proceeds to say that he had wished more than once to come to them, but Satan had prevented him. To us this intervention of Satan may seem a literary device, like the *Deus ex machina* in a Euripidean play : to Paul it was a matter of intense seriousness and bitter reality. For him, as for all Jews interested in apocalyptic belief (p. 16) and for Jesus and all early Christians, the world was full of spiritual beings. God the Father, as supreme creator, ruler and provider, was above all : but God the Father did not usually choose to act directly. He created, with and through his Wisdom or his Logos (Word-Reason), identified with Christ in the fourth Gospel : and he created not only visible objects and beings, but also a multitude of invisible or spiritual beings, commonly called angels. They were created beings, like men : and, though not restricted to the span of human existence or prisoned within bodies, qualitatively they were anything but superior to man. Some of them were good, and acted as protectors of individuals : others were bad, having rebelled against God in one way or another.

The bad angels were still called ' angels ' though the actions ascribed to them resembled those ascribed to *daimonia*, ' evil spirits ' : their ruler was Satan. Paul, however, thinks of angels in general as a mixed category, drawing no invariable distinction between good and bad ; at the last day they will be judged by the Christians (1 Cor. vi. 3). Such supernatural beings were responsible for the death of Jesus. They regarded the Crucifixion as a triumph, whereas in fact it was to prove their downfall. That is what Paul means in 1 Cor. ii. 8, when he says of the wisdom which he reveals : ' None of the Rulers of this Age has learned this ' (that is the function of these powers : they rule this Age in contrast to the Age to Come) ; [1] ' if they had, they would not have crucified the Lord of glory '. At this very point they are putting up a desperate struggle against Paul ; the opposition which he meets, the sufferings which he endures, are due to them and not to the mere human tools which they employ. They received a crushing blow : Christ at his coming will give the *coup de grâce*.

Satan gained the local advantage of preventing Paul's return to Thessalonica and detractors may have suggested that Paul was deserting his converts : in any case, Timothy was sent from Athens to strengthen them and to save them from being led astray from the fold by sufferings, which were the

[1] Cf. Heb. ii. 5 ; 2 Cor. iv. 4, ' the god of this age ', refers to their chief.

destiny of Christians. In due course he brought a good report for which Paul is duly thankful to God, but seems to have indicated the need of some exhortation. So Paul gives a warning against some old pagan habits such as fornication, which did not to these converts as to Jews and to later Christians seem clearly impossible, and an encouragement to be tranquil and carry on their affairs and labour with their own hands. It appears that Paul's teaching of the imminence of the Second Coming had caused some to hold that it was not worth while to take trouble about everyday affairs. Conversion was new and exciting. Converts were very liable to maladjustments and liable to accept other novelties, as in Galatia and at Colossae. The community may have sent him a letter of inquiry. Now Paul was no less convinced than his disciples of the imminence of the new order, in fact of its presence ; but his convictions did not weaken his esteem for normal prudence, or his Jewish regard for the value of toil (cf. p. 21, above).

Two aspects of this Second Coming troubled the Thessalonians. First, what would happen to those of the faithful who died before the Second Coming ? Second, when would that event take place ? Paul answers the first question ' by a word of the Lord ' —probably a remembered saying of Jesus rather than a personal revelation to himself ; we the living who are left (which implies that at this time he was expecting to be one of those left) are not to have any advantage when the Lord comes over those who have fallen on sleep. When the Lord descends, the dead in Christ will rise first and then we, the living who are left, shall be carried simultaneously with them to meet the Lord in the air, and so we shall be altogether with the Lord. Later, in 1 Cor. xv. 12, Paul faces the view ' that there is no resurrection from the dead '. After stating the logical link between the resurrection of the (Christian) dead and the resurrection of Jesus, he states that Christ is risen from the dead as the firstfruits of them that have fallen on sleep, and stresses the parallelism of Adam and Christ (cf. p. 151, above). Each, he says, will rise in his order : Christ as the firstfruits, then they that are Christ's at his presence ; then, it seems, the rest of mankind rise for judgment, and Christ hands over his kingship to the God and Father, and ends all rule and authority and power (that is, all the domination of the angelic powers who prevailed till his first coming in earthly shape and who still prevail over all men save those who are ' in Christ '). Christ must rule until he sets all his enemies, and last of all Death, under his feet. When he has subjected all things to himself, then he will subject himself to the Father, that God may be all in all. This must be so, says Paul, or else Christian life and Christian practice (including vicarious submission to baptism on behalf of the dead) is valueless.

He then explains how the dead will be raised with spiritual bodies ; flesh and blood cannot inherit the

Kingdom of God. 'Behold, I tell you a secret'
—that is, something new which Paul has learned by
revelation and which is now to be told to the world
—we shall not all fall on sleep (Christ will come too
soon for that ; at the same time, the formulation
implies that the Coming is not thought of as quite
so imminent as in 1 Thessalonians) ; we shall all
be changed as soon as the last trumpet sounds ; then
the dead will rise again incorruptible, and we shall
be changed, so that we too may be incorruptible
(cf. Rom. viii. 11). Then will be the fulfilment of
the prophecy that death was swallowed up in victory.
' O death, where is thy victory ? O grave, where is
thy sting ? ' The novelty of this ' secret ' seems
to be that the Messianic victory will be quasi-in-
stantaneous ; the process will be telescoped and the
consummation at once attained.

The second question in 1 Thess. v. is that of times
and seasons. Paul answers that the day of the Lord
comes like a thief in the night, at a time when men
say that they are safe ; both idea and simile are
found in the Gospels (Matt. xxiv. 43 ; Luke xii. 39).
Paul proceeds in his characteristic way to draw moral
inference from a verbal association. ' Thief in the
night ' : yes, but you Thessalonians are not in the
darkness which we associate with night ; you are
sons of light, sons of day. Let us live as the men
of day ; let us be sober, putting on the breastplate
of faith and love and as a helmet the hope of salvation. This is the pregnant metaphor of Isa. lix. 17,

which is further expanded in Wisdom v. 17 ff. (for a more elaborate development see Eph. vi. 14–17). The metaphor of devotion to a cult as a sacred war was familiar in contemporary paganism, but here the arming has a more concrete sense in view of the objective way in which Paul conceived of the forces of evil. There is one further point to notice, the association of this pictorial idea with the faith-love-hope combination (p. 147, above).

A moral imperative is deduced from the special calling of Christians. Herein lies one of the chief differences between Pauline and Stoic ethics : the Stoic deduced that moral imperative from the nature of man as man ; Paul envisaged this in Romans (p. 210, later), but only with the object of showing how paganism could be charged with subjective guilt. We might have supposed that the Pauline theory whereby the believer received the Spirit and is ' in Christ ', would involve the notion that the believer is exempt from the moral struggle. Some of Paul's converts seem, in fact, to have thought so. Nevertheless, his moral exhortations are not simply an abandonment of theory in favour of common sense. He held that the moral imperative was implicit in predestination or election, and that it might be obeyed or not. He was not absolutely certain even of his own future bliss (1 Cor. ix. 27) ; if righteousness can be called a possession, it is also a hope (Gal. v. 5). The Christians were sons of God, but living in an interim condition ; they must be firm, though they need not be frightened (1 Thess. v. 9). They were free—but not in the Stoic sense of being their own masters by living according to ' right law ' : for Paul that would have been the ' righteousness of one's own ' which seemed to him a principal fallacy of Judaism. Freedom from sin was a given freedom from something which was, so to speak, objective and not subjective ; freedom to live in the Spirit and in devotion to the beloved community. Paul and the Stoa agreed, however, in holding that the only personal freedom which mattered was not, as some Corinthians thought, self-expression, but freedom to do the right thing ; furthermore, the Stoa, in its ideal of life ' in conformity with nature ' and of acceptance of Fate involved an attitude which had some analogy to the Pauline idea that man must allow the Spirit to do its work ; but the two employed different approaches.

Paul rejected the notion of a code of conduct obeyed as a code ; that would have seemed to him part of a superseded type of life and incompatible with the new plane on to which Christians were lifted. He could not teach an ascending chain of virtues ; he looked rather to the flowering in the soul of the fruits of the Spirit. Yet this depended on continual endeavour and in this, as in the other Pauline epistles, a passage of exhortation precedes the final greetings and blessings.

The Second Epistle to the Thessalonians also

claims to come from Paul, Silvanus and Timothy and opens with a similar thanksgiving for the community's faith and patience under suffering ; this time Paul uses more elaborately Old Testament language. He then makes a further statement about the Coming of Jesus to prevent their being disturbed by any statement made as though on his authority, that the day of the Lord had already come. To avoid any such misunderstanding Paul, perhaps using a current apocalyptic tract, reminds them of the signs which, as he had taught them (ii. 5), were to precede the end : apostasy, a traditional term which originally meant some widespread lapse of the Jews into paganism just as in the years before the Maccabee revolt ; the manifestation of the Lawless One (an anti-Christ) and his seating of himself in the Temple of God and claiming to be God. This is parallel to the prophecy in Mark xiii. For the moment, as the Thessalonians knew, a restraining power delayed the end, although lawlessness was at work. When the Lawless One should appear, Jesus would destroy him and those who had refused their chance of salvation would have to face judgment.

Paul then resumes his expression of thanks, and asks for the community's prayers and gives further warnings about laziness. Any member of the community who did not hearken to this epistolary injunction was to be designated and kept at arm's length ; he was not to be treated as an enemy, but instructed as a brother.   He writes the greeting in his own hand as a mark of authenticity.

Doubts have, however, often been expressed as to the authenticity of this very letter, largely because, while giving a somewhat different eschatology and being more Jewish and more formal in style, its substance bears so close a resemblance to that of its predecessor. Some who defend it maintain that it is directed to a small group of Jewish Christians in Thessalonica.   On the whole, I incline to regard it as a second letter from Paul to the entire community, written because the first might seem to encourage excessively those whose vivid expectations of an almost immediate Coming had caused them to neglect ' the daily round, the common task '. Paul may well have received a second messenger saying that a number of Thessalonians believed that the day of the Lord had already dawned and that those who were unwilling to work had become more troublesome.

The letters to the Thessalonians give us a notable picture of the human failings of a new community. There were misunderstandings of the doctrine which had been so recently imparted ; there were almost certainly divisions ; the leaders on the spot were perhaps a little too anxious to exercise authority and somewhat lacking in tact, while on the other hand, some of the rank and file, in their confidence in the Spirit which they were said to have received, were reluctant to submit to any direction ; again, moral problems did not disappear overnight.

The chronological sequence of the other ' travel letters ' is open to dispute, but is not a vital question for our present analysis.   We shall begin with Galatians.   Paul reminds those whom he addresses that he has visited them twice.   On the ' South Galatian ' theory the visits could be those of Acts xiv., and the letter could fall before the ' Council of Jerusalem ' ; but, if we are right in accepting the ' North Galatian ' theory (p. 119, above), the two visits to this group of churches will be those of Acts xvi. 6 and xviii. 23, and the letter will belong to the third missionary journey.   The opening of the letter prepares us for the controversy which is its central theme : ' Paul an apostle, not from men nor through man but through Jesus Christ and God the Father who raised him from the dead, and all the brethren with me, unto the churches of Galatia : grace to you and peace from God the Father and our Lord Jesus Christ, who gave himself for our sins, to take us out of the present Evil Age in accordance with the will of our God and Father, to whom be glory for ever and ever.   Amen.'   Paul's authority is questioned, as secondary and derivative : he replies that it is purely divine in its source, from God and Christ.   Also he emphasizes that Christ's death was intended to deliver man, and is wholly and solely sufficient to this end : a supplementary source of grace—the Law—was being preached, and Paul is setting himself to counter this.[1] We can consider only certain main ideas of the letter.

It starts without any thanksgiving to God for the spiritual gifts shown in the lives of the communities addressed (p. 147, above). In Paul's eyes the Galatians are leaving their vocation for a different Gospel, and there cannot be another Gospel. Paul's Gospel came from a direct revelation of Jesus Christ ; he defends his independence from Jerusalem by stating the autobiographic facts already quoted (pp. 64, 105, above), and continues, ' Man is not justified by works of the Law, but only by faith in Jesus Christ.' This applies to Jewish Christians just as much as to Gentile Christians. ' Through Law I died unto Law in order that I may live unto God : and it is no longer I that live, but Christ that lives in me. My present life in the flesh is a life in faith in the Son of God, who loved me and gave himself for me. I do not make null the grace of God : whereas, if righteousness comes through the Law, Christ died for nothing.'

' Righteousness ' and ' justification ' require some explanation. ' Justification ' means ' vindication ', ' acquittal '. In the Old Testament God decides between the righteous and the unrighteous, between his own people and others, and finds in favour of his own. Now there are no human enemies, but there is the danger of God's wrath and the imminence of

[1] iv. 16 perhaps proves some preliminary communication on the matter.

God's judgment. Justification is an anticipation
of a decision of acquittal for the Christians ; it can
be regarded as present or as future, according to
whether Paul thinks of God's eternal decision
anticipating the sentence to be passed at the judgment or of the actual sentence which will be passed.
Righteousness is the quality of God as a judge who
is both just and merciful ; in reference to man it
describes the status of promised justification now
offered to man and the power of overcoming sin
which is also made available through Christ.
Judaism had held that in the Law and in other
dispensations of grace God had given to man the
means by which he could acquire a satisfactory condition. To Paul, as we have seen (p. 69, above),
this seemed to have been disproved by experience.
He held that the Law could not be a means of securing salvation, but was only a condition of living
established for the Jews at a particular time in their
history. It had been established under divine
sanction, but it could not abrogate God's earlier
promise to Abraham ; it had served the historical
function of proving the impossibility of legal
righteousness, for it had actually multiplied trans-
gressions and had led by irresistible logic to the
point at which grace entered life. Now, through
the death of Jesus, God had given both pardon and
the power to live a life which should need no pardon.

We must recall that the authority of the Law, as
here challenged, is the authority of its code as a code

and of legalism as a principle contrasted with faith. Paul never questioned the binding authority of the revelation of God in the Old Testament as a whole, and he appealed from the code to that total revelation. He found there the unique value of faith and he found faith ideally illustrated in the father of the Jews, Abraham himself.

The Galatians ought to have learned as much from the gift of the Spirit (iii. 2). Were their experiences and the miracles done among them to count as nothing ? Compulsory observance of the Law for Gentile Christians would be as pointless as compulsory learning of Hebrew. But in Paul's eyes it was much worse than pointless ; it was wrong and treasonable. The Law involved a curse on any man who violated any of its precepts : this curse had been removed by Christ, who thereby secured for all the blessings of the promise made to Abraham and to his seed, interpreted by Paul as meaning Christ. All Christians, all who had been baptized into Christ, had put on Christ.[1] ' There is not Jew or Gentile, not slave or free, not male or female ; for you are all one person in Christ Jesus. And if you

[1] Baptism and the Eucharist are not ' symbolical ' ; they stand to faith as act or word does to thought ; baptism brings the believer into the unity of the Church and the Eucharist expresses that unity. Nor are these sacraments ' magical ' : their value depends on the effective realization of their ethical implications ; God gives, but man must appropriate.

are of Christ, then you are the seed of Abraham, heirs according to promise ' (iii. 28–29). Paul argues on the basis of the doctrine that the believers are the body of Christ in union with him and one person with him (p. 150, above). Sonship of Abraham is an essential point. Clearly the Judaizing teachers in Galatia had made much of God's promises to Abraham and to his seed (Gen. xvii.) and had insisted that these promises applied only to Jews and to circumcised Gentiles.

' Lo I, Paul, say to you that if you are circumcised, Christ will not avail you. I testify again to every man that is circumcised, that he is under obligation to keep the whole Law ' (v. 2–3). This was no exaggeration ; circumcision meant the acceptance of all the commands. If the Galatian Gentiles who were already baptized Christians, undertook this obligation of the Jewish Law, then there was no help in Christ for them. (Did Paul reflect that they could not be baptized again ?)

The argument moves on, reinforced by appeals to various Old Testament texts ; Paul was meeting his enemies on their own ground, with their own dialectical method. It is characteristic of him that the affection which was so strong an element in his character breaks through the fine ruthlessness of his lengthy arguments. Thus he remembers the goodness shown to him by the Galatians on his first visit, made in sickness ; they would have plucked out their eyes and given them to him ; and he is now in travail with them till Christ be formed in them. If only he could be with them (iv. 12 ff.). ' I trust in the Lord that you will come to the same frame of mind ; but he who confuses you will bear his judgment, whoever he be ' (v. 10).

After the dogmatic argument come the moral inferences. You were called to freedom ; well, you must realize the moral implications of freedom —service through love to one another. The whole Law (about which you have heard so much) is fulfilled in one saying, *Thou shalt love thy neighbour as thyself* (Lev. xix. 18). Both here and in Rom. xiii. 9 Paul recognizes certain ' commands of God ', which in Rom. xiii. 9 are the Ten Commandments summed up in the command of love.

Walk by the Spirit and you shall not fulfil the desire of the flesh ; Spirit and flesh fight.—This dualism is of importance in Paul and recurs in Rom. vii. ; in 1 Cor. ix. 27 we read, ' I buffet my body and bring it into subjection, lest perhaps having preached to others I should myself become a castaway.' The Greeks had been familiar with the idea that the body was an incubus on the soul ; a religious movement of the sixth century B.C., called Orphism, had taught that man included as a divine element an immortal soul, prisoned in the tomb of the body. Largely thanks to Plato, this antithesis had acquired wide popularity and was an appreciable element in the thought of Paul's contemporaries. Paul himself could not be strictly dualist, for he believed that a glorified body would be the mode of the risen life of the Elect ; further, while sympathetic with ascetic discipline, he does not regard it as a way of salvation. The use of the term 'flesh' to express a judgment of value is Hellenistic, but the idea expressed is in all probability the Jewish doctrine of the 'evil impulse' in man. This 'evil impulse' was thought of as not wholly bad, since it led to life and marriage and children and riches ; nor was it irresistible, since the study of the Law and the performance of works of charity were believed to counter it, and it was said that God would suppress it in those who 'nibbled it away'. While asceticism was foreign to Judaism in general, Jewish students were advised to be austere and Jewish saints are described as leading ascetic lives. Nevertheless, Jewish sources do not associate the 'evil impulse' with the flesh ; they set it in the mind and will, and externally Paul hellenizes.

The works of the flesh include sins which go beyond the realm of the physical—idolatry, enmities, jealousy, rivalry, divisions, factions. Paul's implicit moral code develops along the line of works of the flesh and fruits of the Spirit. Paul never abandoned his belief that the Spirit was the sole ultimate criterion, and that the virtues were a natural flowering of the Spirit in men's lives, but by this classification he was able to incorporate in his own scheme the handy lists of virtues and vices which had been developed by Hellenistic Judaism and popular philosophy.

In any case, the way of escape was to be found not in self-discipline nor in an ascending chain of virtues which were, so to speak, conquests made by the individual, but in the guidance of the Spirit and in the allied sense of the paramount importance of the community and of its life in mutual service. ' They that are of the Christ, Jesus, have crucified the flesh with its dispositions and desires ', and this leads again to the moral imperative, ' If we live by the Spirit, let us also walk by the Spirit ', ultimately, we shall reap as we have sown. This may seem to be directed against error of a type opposite to that which is the main problem of Galatians, in fact against error of the type which we shall find at Corinth. This inference should not be pressed, because the pattern of exhortation is that which is normal in Paul, and it does not justify specific conclusions. After some advice of this type, Paul reverts to the circumcision issue. The advocates of circumcision in reality seek to escape persecution : even those who are by way of submitting to the rite do not really keep the Law—that is, they do not keep it with the rigour and precision which Paul as Pharisee had learned as the standard (vi. 13).

This is extremely important, for the reason that it has been urged that the Judaizers in Galatia had been influenced, not by envoys from Jerusalem, but by contact with and pressure from local Jews. Such pressure no doubt existed, but we must note, first, the parallel to Paul's charge against Peter (ii. 14); secondly, the imputation of motive ' in order that they may not be persecuted by reason of the Cross of Christ '. This fits perfectly the situation of Jewish Christians at Jerusalem.[1] The first serious persecution which they suffered arose out of the quasi-Gentile criticism of the Law and the Temple by Stephen. Things were no doubt better now : James the Just was in such good standing that his death in 62, as a result of the fanaticism of the High Priest of the time, was very ill received by good Jews. If the Pauline mission could be curbed and brought into line, the Jewish Christians would be fairly secure from interference. The *pseudapostoloi*, ' false apostles ', of 2 Cor. xi. 13, can hardly be explained otherwise than as emissaries from a party at Jerusalem. Paul's demonstration of his personal authority to teach was a powerful argument against them and only against them [2]—unless possibly

[1] And at many centres of the Dispersion.

[2] For another view, cf. J. H. Ropes, *The Singular Problem of the Epistle to the Galatians* (Harvard University Press, 1929), well criticized by J. M. Creed, *Journal of Theological Studies*, 31 (1930), pp. 421 ff. No ' North Galatians ' are mentioned in Acts xx. 4. This is not too secure a basis for argument—the Galatians might, for instance, have sent their delegate directly to Jerusalem : but it is possible that the absence of evidence for early Christian groups in ' North Galatia ' is due to a complete success on the part of Paul's adversaries : the original

against emissaries from the Jewish Christians at Antioch who had abandoned Paul (Gal. ii. 13).

To return, these men, says Paul, wish to circum-cise you in order that they may glory in your flesh : such glorying is a wrong thing : ' may it not be mine to glory save in the Cross of our Lord Jesus Christ, through whom the world is crucified to me and I to the world. For neither circumcision nor uncircumcision is anything : only a new creation is anything.' Only the substitution of the new order of men who have died and risen with Christ has any meaning.

' For the rest, let no man trouble me : for I bear in my body the branding marks of Jesus ' : that is to say, ' I am in a supreme degree the slave of Jesus, his property to deal with me as he wills : no one else in the world has any claim upon me.'

converts may have accepted all the requirements of Judaism and passed into the world of proselytes, losing their effective power to attract new converts and losing also contact with Christian groups.

CHAPTER VII

THE TRAVEL LETTERS : II. CORINTHIANS

WHEN Paul wrote to the Galatians, he had but one problem, though it was of the most serious type. His Corinthian correspondence handled a multiplicity of questions, all familiar to his readers and to him, and he passes from one to another with a rapidity and an elusiveness which are often baffling. The task of interpretation is therefore difficult, particularly since the Second Epistle seems to combine portions of two or three letters. Nevertheless, in spite of the gaps in our knowledge, the two Epistles are historical documents of the first order of importance, not only for the history of Christianity, but also for the general cultural and religious conditions of the time. The short life of Corinthian Christianity produced a most remarkable diversity of development ; ecstasy and spiritual pride, asceticism and lust, scruples and self-justifying indulgence, loyalty and partisanship.

The reconstruction of the sequence of events and letters here accepted is as follows :

(1) A letter to which Paul refers in 1 Cor.

v. 9, written at some time after the departure
from Corinth recorded in Acts xviii. 18 and
intended to warn the Corinthians against being
a little too much with the world, late and soon.
2 Cor. vi. 14–vii. 1 may be a fragment of this
letter. It seems to have led to misunderstandings,
whether sincere or not.

(2) Then Paul, during his long stay at Ephesus,
received various questions and reports, which
made him anxious, but not unduly anxious; he
expected that the Corinthian church would hasten
to set its house in order. So he wrote 1 Corinthians, which Titus may well have carried. Then
distressing news reached Paul, and he revisited
Corinth and found things in a most unsatisfactory
state. 'False apostles' had come into the community and were making the gravest charges against
Paul, and there was acute personal unpleasantness.
Paul returned to Ephesus in sorrow and wrote

(3) A letter of sadness and anger, probably
carried by Titus; 2 Cor. x.–xiii. is very likely a
part of this letter;[1] in these chapters Paul demands obedience, replies to charges against his
character, apostolic authority, and spiritual gifts,

[1] The reader should, however, bear in mind that
Lietzmann and other eminent critics defend the literary
unity of 2 Corinthians, and that others accept the hypothesis that chapters x.–xiii. are part of a still later letter,
which assumes that the conflict sharpened after the writing
of 2 Cor. i.–ix.

and expresses the deepest grief over widespread moral laxity. Titus was able to return with better news, and in profound thankfulness and great kindness Paul wrote

(4) A letter of reconciliation, which is 2 Cor. i.–ix., sent after open hostility has caused him to leave Ephesus, on a journey through Macedonia (perhaps from Philippi).

We may now consider (2), (3) and (4). 1 Corinthians starts with a greeting, in which Paul couples with his own name that of Sosthenes, and strikes the note of Christian unity, and proceeds to thank God for the grace given to the Corinthian church. Then he starts a series of topics, dealt with in order. First, let there not be divisions among them. Each of them is saying, ' I am of Paul ', ' I am of Apollos ', ' I am of Cephas [1]', ' I am of Christ ' ; that is to say, people who are disciples of Paul, Apollos, and Cephas respectively are in definite rivalry : the ' party of Christ ' probably represents a group who claimed special personal revelation (perhaps like Paul's) and guidance by the Spirit and consequent emancipation, and a possible allusion to them has been detected in 2 Cor. x. 7. To Paul this is shocking. There was no question—as in Galatia—of another Gospel, which is no Gospel : there were imperfect Christians, no imperfect types of Christianity. Apollos was clearly on good terms with Paul (p. 200,

[1] i.e. Peter. Cf. p. 111, above.

later), but his disciples may have spoken of Paul's teaching in an unflattering way.

Secondly, there is the question of wisdom (i. 18–iv. 21). Paul was disquieted with attitudes at Corinth, which he reproves, without needing to state what they were. Conversion has various effects on people, and one of them is a new sense of power. When a man is converted to Christianity to-day, a tradition based on the long centuries of experience guides and regulates his instincts. Jewish Christians had a comparable tradition ; Gentile Christians had not. Many of the converts, convinced that they were on a new plane of life, felt that they could do anything : they were kings (iv. 8), they were in the Spirit, they were dead to the flesh and emancipated—so that their physical conduct might seem to them a matter of indifference ; they were altogether superior to the unchanged men around them.

They included ' not many wise after the flesh, not many powerful, not many well born ' (i. 26). Could not the secret dreams of grandeur which many of them had hugged be now fulfilled ? We can infer some of these dreams from the magical papyri, which tell us the things which men thought that they could thus compel the gods to give them. ' I pray to the Lord, that I may not fail, nor be the objects of plots, nor take any noxious potion, nor fall into embarrassments or trouble of subsistence, but receive and obtain from thee, life, health, fame, riches, power, strength, good luck, loveliness, favour with all men and all women, victory over all men and all women '; 'that I alone may enter heaven and see everything '; 'I will not allow any god or any goddess to give oracles until I learn the things in the souls of all men, Egyptians, Syrians, Greeks, Ethiopians, and every race and every people, who question me and meet me, whether they speak or are silent, that I may tell them their past and present and future, and may know their crafts and lives and occupations and works and names.'[1]

The Corinthians could not pretend to themselves that they had acquired birth, wealth, and power ; the other things which connoted superiority in the ancient world were eloquence and wisdom. If you did not have them, your mental picture of their importance might be even the more highly coloured—like certain popular notions to-day of the possibility of physical and even social science. The philosopher was commonly regarded as a ' divine man ', credited with the power to work miracles, and associated with occult arts. The Corinthians wished to enter this charmed circle.

Paul seeks to remedy some such unhealthy state of mind. He replies that he has his type of wisdom—as distinct from the signs sought by

[1] S. Eitrem, *Papyri Osloenses*, I, p. 27 ; K. Preisendanz, *Papyri graecae magicae*, iv., 434 ; v., 286 ff.

the Jews and the wisdom sought by the Greeks :
it is God's hidden pre-ordained wisdom, the plan
of Christ's descent and death to wreck the rule
of angelic powers (p. 153, above). That wisdom
can be apprehended only by the spiritual man,
for he alone has the organ whereby it can be
apprehended, namely, the Spirit of God, the mind
of Christ. Paul could not give the Corinthians
teaching on this level : they were not equal to it,
for they were fleshly ; and they are not now
equal to it, for they are fleshly, as is shown by their
factiousness and rivalry.[1] That they can pit Paul
against Apollos shows that they do not understand
that the work is God's, and men are but helpers,
and helpers in virtue of God's grace given to
them, privileged to share in building the sanctuary
of God—that is, the congregation. No wisdom
can be obtained without an abnegation of worldly
wisdom. Everything—we teachers, the universe,
life, death, things present, things to come—is
yours, but you are Christ's, and Christ is God's,
and God will be the sole judge of all of us. Hence
do not indulge in self-satisfaction over any gifts
which you may have : we Apostles, at least, have
learnt humility in the school of humiliation.

Thirdly, very bad fornication, worse than Gentiles tolerate, is reported from Corinth ; a man

---

[1] Consistency with Rom. viii. 9 would perhaps require
that the Corinthians are not availing themselves fully of
the divine gift.

living with his father's wife, and apparently the Corinthian church has not excommunicated the offender, and even, in its curious freedom of the ' Spirit ', seems rather pleased with itself. This offender is to be handed over to Satan for the destruction of his flesh, in order that his spirit may be saved in the day of the Lord. The decision is very illuminating. Not only does it foreshadow the ecclesiastical discipline of excommunication, but also it shows that the principle of authority and jurisdiction dominated the Pauline communities just as much as it did those Jewish Christian groups which inherited the discipline and ' ban ' of the synagogue. Further, Paul assumed that a sentence passed by himself and the community would certainly be ratified by God.

The community had to live in the world as it was, but it must look to its internal standards and must not have fellowship, must not even eat, with any so-called brother who was vicious. It must judge those within ; God would judge those without. Sexual morality was a very serious thing in Paul's eyes.

The mention of judgment leads to the fourth point. Christians must not go to law with one another before heathen courts. To Jews domestic jurisdiction was familiar in the cities of the Dispersion. Hellenistic pagan religious guilds had no such custom : their only prohibition had been on lawsuits arising out of differences *at meetings* between members. The Jewish reason for trying their own cases had been the wish to settle them in accordance with Jewish law. Paul supplies a special reason why Christians should act thus. The saints are to judge the universe : this judgment, says Paul, extends even to angels—that is, to the whole world of spirit-beings.[1] And no evil men will inherit the Kingdom. You were such, ' But you were washed, you were sanctified, you were justified by the Name of the Lord Jesus Christ and by the Spirit of our God ' (vi. 11). Baptism, the gift of the Spirit, anticipatory acquittal for the Judgment—they are all aspects of the same thing.

This brings us back to the third point, fornication. ' All things are permitted unto me (perhaps quoted from what the Corinthians said), but not all things are expedient. All things are permitted unto me, but I will not be dominated by any thing. Meats for the belly and the belly for meats ; but God will bring both to naught.' From Paul's standpoint many Corinthians thought too much of new spiritual prerogatives (which he did not wish to deny) and too little of moral duty. Eating was in the last analysis a matter of indifference except where it involved the feelings or conscience of others ; but sex was not. Our bodies have to be considered in the light of their

[1] This idea lives side by side with the other—that Christians, like everyone else, have to face judgment.

destiny at the resurrection of our physical union with Christ and of the statement, ' Your body is a temple of the Holy Spirit in you, which you have from God '.

After these four points Paul comes to issues raised in a letter to him from the community. The first was : should a man have sexual relations with his wife ? The question was raised perhaps partly because of expectations of the Coming, but partly also perhaps because of an idea that abstinence had an occult value in some pagan circles. Paul replies, expressing a personal conviction that abstinence is the ideal but emphasizing that concession is far better than sin, and that either party must satisfy the other's needs if felt. So with the unmarried and widows, it is good for them to remain even as Paul ; but it is better to marry than to be consumed with desire. In all this, as in the approximation to a new ethical code (p. 157, above), we see Paul's common sense and practical judgment. As for divorce, a woman is not to leave her husband, and, if she does, is to remain unmarried or be reconciled : a husband is not to divorce his wife. That he gives as the Lord's command (cf. Mark x. 11–12) ; it was a difficult doctrine for pagans and for Jews. Paul gives a personal direction, for which he does not claim the Lord's authority, that a Christian is not to leave an unbelieving marriage partner : if the partner goes, well and good ; otherwise, there is the hope of a sanctification of the believer by contact with the ' body of Christ ' (p. 150, above).

These considerations lead on to the statement of a general principle. ' Only as the Lord has given to each, in the condition in which God has called each, so let him walk. And so I order in all the churches.' Once more Paul gives an absolute order, and states it three times in eight verses, with illustrations. Whether you are circumcised or uncircumcised when ' called ', stay as you were : if you are a slave, make no effort to be free. Paul has no ' social Gospel '.

A second matter, presumably raised by the Corinthians in the letter brought to Paul, now follows—the problem of ' virgins ' ; it apparently relates to a curious custom whereby men were spiritually betrothed to virgins and even lived with them without having physical relations ; difficulties were liable to arise. Once more, Paul prefers continence, but regards the concession of ordinary matrimony as right if it is the way to avoid sin. In the same manner, he permits the re-marriage of a widow ' only in the Lord ', that is, presumably, to a Christian for the prevention of moral evil.

The third topic in this series is that of meats offered to idols. In the ancient world many people seldom ate meat except after a sacrifice, which was a social occasion to which you invited your friends. Certain portions of the sacrifice were the priest's portion, and, as he received not only these but also similar portions from public sacrifices—or an equivalent in cash—there was plenty to sell in the market, and any meat sold in the market might have been dedicated in the first instance to a pagan deity. From the standpoint of a Jew or of a Jewish Christian, it was wholly inacceptable on two grounds : first, this possibility of an association with idolatry ; second, the certainty that it would not have been ' bled ' and would have the blood that is the life in it.[1] We have already seen how the Jewish Christian group tried to enforce on Gentile Christians absolute abstinence from all such meat, and how Paul could not regard the decree as binding (p. 117, above). Here he treats the problem purely on general principles, without any reference to the decisions of others or to the Jewish Law.

His argument in effect looks back to the discussion of ' wisdom ' (p. 175, above), and forward to the praise of faith, hope, and love, particularly love, as superior to so-called ' spiritual gifts ' (p. 195, later). ' Now concerning meats offered to idols, we are aware that we all have knowledge. Knowledge puffs up (which specifically recalls iv. 18), but love edifies. If a man thinks he has knowledge of anything, he has not yet come to

---

[1] As Lietzmann remarks, the Christians were not sure enough of this world's continuance to start their own butchers' shops.

know as he ought to know : if any one loves God, he is known by God.' Clearly 'knowledge' is a battle-cry : Paul allows that Christians have a 'knowledge', an understanding of mysteries hidden from Jew and Gentile alike ; but this 'knowledge' is imperfect, whereas a deliberate set of the will to the love of God and man is rewarded by a result which *is* perfect. The advocates of knowledge maintained that an idol was nothing, and that therefore the dedication of food to an idol was a transaction without significance, which in all logic ought not to affect the eatability of meat. Paul allows the premise as valid, but argues that some of the conclusions drawn are inacceptable. Some people in sheer habit will still eat such meats actually as meats offered to idols : their conscience being weak is defiled —they have not reached the full stature of Christian freedom, and the action seems to them idolatry and is for them idolatry. If they see you, who have knowledge, reclining in a pagan temple and eating—whether food from an ordinary sacrifice, or food distributed to the members of a pagan cult society—they will be encouraged to do likewise : and *for them* such eating will be idolatry. In that case, for the sake of food which in any case will not help your soul, you are endangering them. (There is a saying ascribed to Jesus in the 'Western text' of Luke vi. 5 : 'On the same day he saw one working on the Sabbath and said unto him, O man, if thou knowest what thou dost, thou art blessed ; if thou dost not know, thou art accurst and a transgressor of the Law ' —which involves a similar principle.) Paul nowhere shows greater wisdom.

In effect, he asks the Corinthians with ' knowledge ' to surrender what he allows to be their right, whenever the moral good of others demands it. He reinforces his claim by pointing to his own example. Although he is free, an Apostle, a witness of Jesus our Lord, the founder of the Corinthian community, he does not take a wife around or live at the expense of the community —both indisputably rights of his, the latter guaranteed by an order of the Lord (cf. Luke x. 7) : he did in part accept help from the Philippians and from other communities (p. 223, later : 2 Cor. xi. 8–10). We shall see later (p. 201) that this self-denial of Paul was by some construed as an admission that he had no such rights. That issue is not raised here : instead, Paul proceeds to another moral inference. He, Paul, is like an athlete in constant training, always disciplining his body, lest he himself become a castaway (p. 166, above).

They too must take warning. If he is on his guard, they should be on theirs. All our fathers —that is, all of the historical Jewish nation whose heirs the Christians are—were ' baptized into Moses ' in the cloud and in the sea : all of them

ate the same supernatural food and drank the same
supernatural drink, from the rock which accompanied them and which was Christ : but God
was not well pleased with the greater part of
them, and they were laid low in the desert. The
redemption of Israel out of Egypt had commonly
been regarded as a foreshadowing of the expected
redemption of Israel from the present evil world-
order. So here the Jewish people on its pilgrim-
age to the Promised Land is treated as a type
foreshadowing the Christians on the way to the
Kingdom. The cloud that went before them,
and the crossing of the Red Sea, correspond to
baptism ; the manna, which Philo explained as
God's Word from heaven and of which Exodus
xvi. 15 says, ' This is the bread which the Lord
hath given you to eat ' (words which could seem
strangely parallel to those of Jesus at the Last
Supper), and the water from the rock struck by
Moses (which, according to a well-known Jewish
story, accompanied them on their wanderings),
correspond to the Eucharist. They were God's
elect, with divine privileges analogous to the
Christian rites ; but neither election nor privileges awaited them at all when they transgressed
the moral law, and ' these things were written for
the instruction of us, upon whom the ends of
the ages have come '. The difficulty which Paul
here encountered arose out of the Gentile origin
of their converts. The Gentile world had initia-

tions : now these were solemn ceremonies, and the initiate was expected to be put into a proper state of mind and sometimes exhorted to continue in a proper state of conduct : at the same time, in general the ceremony was thought to achieve its end without reference to the subsequent conduct of the initiate. The Pauline teaching that the baptized person came to be ' in Christ ' was particularly liable to lead to misunderstandings of this type as well as to the general assumption of a position of superiority.

At this point Paul returns with new force to the question of idolatry. It is a danger, he says, in a comprehensive sense. Think of your Eucharist. ' The cup of blessing which we bless, is it not the joint participation [1] of the blood of Christ ? The bread which we break, is it not the joint participation [1] of the body of Christ ? For we, the many, are one bread, one body : [2] since we all share the one bread.' A meal takes character from its setting : so does the Jewish eating of the meat from a sacrifice. Paul grants that meat offered to an idol is in itself nothing, that the idol is nothing ; but sacrifice has an intention : it is offered to *daimonia*, ' evil spirits ', and not to God ; and I do not wish you to enter

[1] Some translate ' fellowship '.
[2] Professor Dodd suggests that the meaning may be ' because there is one loaf, we, the many (partaking of it), are one body '.

into a similar relationship with *daimonia*.—To eat meat offered to idols *as* meat offered to idols was clearly out of bounds ; in the Old Testament analogy, idolatry was one of the sins which had brought destruction on the Jews. *Daimonia* cannot hurt you ; but your deliberate contact with them is an insult to God, and God's wrath is dangerous.

God matters ; legalism does not, and morbidity is not virtue. So you may eat anything sold in the market or offered to you at a Gentile dinner, without scruple. But if someone says to you, ' This comes from a sacrifice,' then do not eat it : to do so would involve acceptance of idolatry ; that is the effect which it would have on the conscience or consciousness of others (in particular, ' weaker ' Christians), and your criterion, like Paul's, must be the glory of God and the advantage of others.

We pass now to questions of church order. Women must be veiled in church (theological reasons are given). Paul as a Jew had a predisposition in favour of this, but it is possible also that he wished to avoid anything like Dionysiac enthusiasm. Further, Corinthian habits at the common meal or Eucharist needed correction.[1] The Corinthians had divisions and class distinc-

[1] I Cor. xi. 17 ff. This passage perhaps means that every formal meeting of the community included the common meal.

tions ; each took his own food and some fared
ill and some too well. They could gratify their
own tastes at home. ' I received from the Lord,[1]
what I also handed on to you ' (but not apparently
with such rigour that there could be no misunderstanding : they could confuse the Eucharist
with a meal, in a way in which they could not
confuse baptism with a bath), ' that the Lord
Jesus in the night in which he was betrayed
took bread, and having given thanks, broke it
and said, This is my body for you : do this (*or*,
you do this) for a remembrance of me. So likewise after supper [2] he took the cup, saying, This
cup is the new Covenant in my blood : do this
(*or*, you do this) whenever you drink it, for a
remembrance of me. In fact, whenever you eat
this bread and drink the cup, you proclaim the
Lord's death, until he comes. Accordingly, whoever eats the bread or drinks the cup of the Lord
unworthily, will be liable for the body and the
blood of the Lord. And let a man examine
himself and only so eat of the bread and drink
of the cup : for he that eateth and drinketh,
eateth and drinketh judgment on himself, not
distinguishing the body. For this reason many
among you are sick and infirm, and a number

[1] The phrase probably implies ' through a tradition
coming from those who were present on that occasion '.
[2] The order of proceedings is : breaking of bread,
eating in general, blessing of Cup.

fall on sleep. If we applied moral tests to ourselves, we should not be judged : when we are
judged by the Lord we are disciplined, in order
that we may not share in the condemnation awaiting
the world.'

In considering this passage, which shows that
the Corinthian community, though sizeable, had
a room in which it could meet, let us start with
the end. Sickness and death were not uncommon,
and Paul perhaps held them, as he did the probable
bodily fate of the man handed over to Satan (p. 177,
above), to be a chastisement which might make
satisfaction for post-baptismal sin and qualify the
sufferer to enjoy that share in bliss which he was
in danger of forfeiting. Now the earlier community at Jerusalem probably connected the
Christian meal of fellowship with the general
table-fellowship of the disciples with Jesus and
with the hope of future table-fellowship with the
Messiah (p. 58, above). Paul retained the second
idea, but for the first he substituted a connection
with the Last Supper in particular. Of this there
was a tradition at Jerusalem ; though the words
which Jesus was said to have then uttered had
for Paul a peculiar meaning, the Eucharist does
not appear in Paul's controversies with Jewish
Christians—any more than baptism, to which also
he attached a special meaning. At that Last
Supper one man, Judas, reclined under the shadow
of ultimate condemnation : ' well for that man,

if he had not been born' (Mark xiv. 21). The linkage of the Eucharist with that Supper involved solemnity and danger. So did its description as 'proclaiming the death of Christ'. The Corinthians, like the Jews leaving Egypt (p. 184), had responsibilities which corresponded to their privileges.

The Eucharistic elements could be spoken of as 'spiritual (i.e. supernatural) food' and 'spiritual drink' (1 Cor. x. 3–4) : but that aspect is not here developed, as it is in the Fourth Gospel. 'The participation in (or fellowship of) the blood of Christ', 'the participation in (or fellowship of) the body of Christ', do not state that those present receive individually the body and the blood as new if recurrent gifts, but that they participate in his body (which probably means his glorified body of the resurrection, but would naturally suggest also the other sense of 'body of Christ'), and they participate in his blood, whereby his life was offered to God. Paul's form of words, 'the new covenant in my blood', exactly expresses the transaction ; taking the Cup represents participation in the covenant. Thus the corporeal solidarity of Christians with Christ was expressed in communion, just as it had been attained and realized in 'dying and rising with Christ' (p. 240, later). On Paul's theory there can be no securing in this way of the 'meat and drink of the soul' : Christian life for him meant an increasing realiza-

tion of the holiness already placed in man to use ;
not an increasing growth of holiness as a result
of appropriate nourishment. (The manna and
the water from the rock took the place of other
sustenance, and kept the Israelites alive ; they
were a privilege, but they did not confer any
special virtues upon them.) The sinner did not
' distinguish the body '. The word for distinguish,
diakrino, is the word used of distinguishing *pneumata*
or various spirits which offered inspiration. The
sinner did not apprehend the significance of the
body—the one bread which was Christ's body
and implied a present reality, a symbol of Christ
and of the Church. Just as in the problem of
meats offered to idols, the meaning ascribed to
an act determines its ethical character. He incurred a danger like that of the Galatians, who
did not realize the significance of their baptism
(p. 164, above). The whole Pauline scheme of
thought turns on divine action, which gives to
man through appointed channels the possibility
of life in the Spirit ; once this possibility had
been accepted, to throw it away was perilous.

Two essential points are shared by this Pauline
picture with the Last Supper as recorded in the
Gospels, and with the early Christian rite described
in the *Teaching of the Twelve Apostles* (p. 55,
above) : the ' blessing ' of cup and bread in
Jewish style, and the expectation of the Second
Coming. What calls for explanation is the pres-

ence of the words, ' This do . . .' or ' You do this . . .' They are not found in Mark or Matthew or in the shorter textual form of Luke (the longer form being in all probability secondary and due to conflation with the text of Paul). The evidence is entirely against Jesus having said them, or having thought of any repetition. He probably anticipated that the Last Things would at once follow upon his death, and yet Paul professes to quote actual words on the basis of which he proceeds to argue. On this point Paul may have thought he had a special revelation : alternatively, we may recall that he almost certainly did not possess any written Sayings of Jesus. He had the memory of what he had been told, and our memory of words is liable to become fused with our interpretation of them, and with all the associations which have gathered around them in our minds.[1] So in Gal ii. 14 ff., Paul's answer to Cephas passes gradually into what are simply reflections addressed to the Galatians.

What was in Paul's mind ? The disciples at Jerusalem knew of the Last Supper at which the

[1] Paul's other differences from Mark are of the type which naturally arises from memory : ' for you ' is attached to the saying about the bread, to make its meaning clear ; ' my blood of the covenant ' becomes ' the new covenant in my blood ' (unless we accept the view that the Pauline form is the older and the Marcan assimilated to Exod. xxiv. 8 ; ' poured out for many ' is omitted).

Twelve had been present, as something belonging to the days of the Master, and practised their communal meals as something belonging to the days of subsequent readjustment. Paul was introduced to the communal meals, probably at Damascus, and heard of the Last Supper and drew his inference. The point was clear to him from then, and he could not but feel that Jesus so intended it. Further, the repetition of the Last Supper is for him part of the scheme of edification : the eating and drinking together of a Christian community must always bring Jesus into their minds, until he come again. Pagans often left bequests for funerary meals, or distributions of wine or oil, in order to keep their names fresh in the minds of the living ; for the Judaism in which Paul grew up one of the most solemn moments of the year was the Passover meal eaten in memory of the deliverance of Israel and preserving for ever the hour of salvation (p. 53, above). The word translated as ' proclaim ' does not involve any sort of dramatic re-presentation of the death of Jesus, such as we find later. At the same time, this Pauline view lies behind all subsequent development. Resting as it did on an undisputed tradition of the Last Supper, it could not but triumph, and necessarily brought with itself the gradual differentiation of the Eucharist from the communal meal.

Three further observations must be made. The

Teaching of the Twelve, speaking of the Sunday ceremony which it has described, provides (c. 14) for previous confession of sins 'that your sacrifice may be pure . . . For this is the sacrifice mentioned by the Lord' (with a quotation from Malachi i. 11). The corporate prayers of the Eucharist, apparently even in a surviving pre-Pauline form,[1] are thus treated as the Christian counterpart of the old sacrifices of the Temple; this line of thought is further developed by later writers. In Paul, on the other hand, the Eucharist is not so regarded, and the equivalent of the old sacrifices is right conduct, the offering of the body as a living sacrifice, the service of reason (Rom. xii. 1), or the faith of the Philippians (Phil. ii. 17),[2] just as to James i. 27 pure and undefiled worship is the visiting of orphans and widows in their affliction and the keeping of oneself unspotted from the world. Even for John, in spite of his elaboration of Eucharistic piety, the worship of the future is to be 'in spirit and truth' (iv. 23). Paul ascribes to himself a quasi-priestly function in Rom. xv. 16, but in relation to the Gentiles, as an acceptable offering hallowed by the Holy Spirit.

[1] Some scholars regard this phrase as referring to what we think of as a normal Eucharist and not to the ceremony discussed p. 55, above ; this seems improbable. The reader should bear in mind that the Greek word for 'sacrifice' covers bloodless as well as animal offerings.

[2] But in Col. ii. 12–13 baptism is treated as analogous to circumcision.

Secondly, the sacrificial idea, as linked to the Eucharist in the *Teaching*, is not inferred from what Jesus said of the 'covenant'. Thirdly, neither Paul nor the Epistle to the Hebrews, nor any other Christian text of the first two centuries as known to me, drew any theological inference from the 'covenant' saying, and even Irenaeus makes no use of it in discussing the relation of the redemptive acts of Jesus to the covenants of the Old Dispensation or to Jer. xxxi. 33. The 'new' covenant is related directly to the death of Jesus and not incidentally also to the Last Supper.

These observations illustrate an important aspect of the Eucharist. It was on a very different footing from baptism. Baptism from the beginning is a central fact in theology as well as in corporate life; Paul does not hesitate to draw theological inferences from it and it comes into the Creeds. Although the full phrase 'I believe . . . in one baptism (of repentance) for the remission of sins' does not appear in a formal Creed till the fourth century, Eph. iv. 5 has 'one Lord, one faith, one baptism' in a creed-like formulation, and 'forgiveness of sins', which implies baptism and is in fact an equivalent, figures in the 'old Roman Creed' and in the so-called 'Epistle of the Apostles', a document not much later than the middle of the second century. Of course, Creeds, as formulated, are baptismal Creeds; even so, this remains significant. The Eucharist is never mentioned in a Creed ; [1] its place was in the corporate life of the Church and not in its theology. The 'covenant' saying of Jesus remains as an acted parable or symbol which from the time of Paul was associated with the origin of the Christian rite of fellowship. In the fourth Gospel the Eucharist is given a theology as the sustenance of those reborn by baptism. This is part of a change of emphasis. As the 'wrath to come' faded into the distance, the transformation of man's nature (which is what John means by 'eternal life') became more important than man's deliverance from an imminent peril, and therefore Incarnation became relatively much more important in comparison with Atonement. Nevertheless, even with this shift of emphasis, the Eucharist remained the object of piety and not of controversy.

After the discussion of the Eucharist, Paul proceeds to deal with manifestations of the Spirit. The Corinthians connected the Spirit mainly with the ability to speak with tongues (that is, to utter, in ecstasy, words and sounds with no intelligible meaning), prophecy (the delivering of inspired and yet intelligible messages to the Church) and 'knowledge' of the secrets of religion. Such

[1] Unless the phrase commonly translated 'the communion of saints' means, as some maintain, 'participation in the sacraments'; but to me this seems unlikely.

manifestations were likely to appeal to Gentiles of their social standing ; ecstasy, prophecy and miracles were highly valued by the less educated, and the new religion appeared to make them available and to enable every man to be his own prophet.

Paul does not deny the reality and validity of these spiritual gifts ; in fact he regards their range as very extended ; 'no one can say, Jesus is Lord, save by the Holy Spirit' (xii. 3). He insists that other and more useful accomplishments are gifts of the Spirit no less than the obviously miraculous manifestations. All the activities of the community are due to the Spirit, and the unity of the Spirit corresponds to the unity of the body of Christ into which all Christians, Jew or Gentile, slave or free, were baptized. We have our several duties and functions, but all a part of the whole.

The Corinthians are in danger of losing their sense of perspective. 'And I show unto you a more excellent way', the way stated in chapter xiii. as the way of love, *agape*. *Agape* is a kindliness and a warmth of affection and consideration which has a quality as of spontaneity but involves a deliberate and yet uncalculating set of the will, a conscious determination to think the best of fellow Christians and to do the most for them, bending without condescending. It is wholly different from *eros*, overmastering passion which, while supreme, dominates and supersedes the will, and which does not carry with itself considerateness. *Agape* is a quality of Christian life without which other gifts and accomplishments, even such gifts of the Spirit as have just been described, leave their possessor nothing worth : further, it is a quality which will remain in the New Age when men will no more need the spiritual props of present life. It is also an attitude towards Christ and God and a quality of Christ and of God (Rom v. 8, viii. 35, 39 : 2 Cor. xiii. 13), and the love of God is poured forth in the hearts of Christians through the Holy Spirit (Rom. v. 5 ; cf. xv. 30). Like the righteousness of God imparted to man, it is a divine attribute which grace makes available ; it resembles that righteousness also in that here again the indicative involves an imperative. For Paul it deserves the name of spiritual fully as much as does the ability to speak with tongues. ' And now remain these three things, faith, hope, *agape* '—the triad which we have met before (p. 147, above) ; and *agape* is greater than the other two. In this chapter Paul, by a flash of intuitive generalization, has left his most fruitful utterance ; the style keeps pace with the thought, and there is a serene elevation. It is as though he had dictated chapters i.–xii., dealing methodically with the questions which presented themselves at Corinth : and then, as it were in a new morning, he felt moved to put the whole issue on a higher plane. The thought is normal Pauline thought, but the form is unique.

Returning to the main theme, Paul emphasizes that prophecy is more useful than speaking with tongues, because prophecy edifies. He argues at some length. Clearly it was very important that Corinthian Christianity should not degenerate into imitative hysterics, and yet Paul could not ' quench the Spirit ' ; he could not deny that even those ' manifestations of the Spirit ' which seemed to him of less practical utility than others were manifestations of the Spirit. The Corinthians were very proud of their ' gifts ', and they could, of course, claim that their ' gifts ' were among the recognized and regular phenomena of the Spirit. Paul handles the situation very delicately, pointing out, for instance, that praying in ' tongues ' leaves the mind without fruit, and a prayer with the mind should be added : a psalm with the mind should be added to a psalm with the Spirit (xiv. 14–15). Again, what if an unbeliever enters their assembly, and everyone is talking with tongues, will he not say that they are mad ? But if everyone is prophesying, his heart will be touched, and he will be forced to acknowledge that God is among them (xiv. 23–25). This is an instructive picture of one way in which new members came to join a Christian community. They might visit out of pure curiosity, and then be converted. Let there be a proper balance in your meeting, with its (Christian) psalms, instructions, revelations, tongues, and interpretation of tongues : not more than two or three speakers with tongues, and they only if there is one who can interpret : not more than two or three prophets, and one to interpret : only one prophet to talk at a time. The spirits of prophets are subject to prophets—that is, as Harnack says, to their ' reflecting will '. No women are to talk at all in formal church meetings.[1] Let any prophet or ' spiritual man recognize that what Paul writes is a command of the Lord : if he does not know that, God does not know him '.

Paul then summarizes the Gospel, ' that Christ died for our sins according to the Scriptures, and that he was buried and that he rose again on the third day according to the Scriptures ' lists the appearances of the Risen Lord (p. 41 above), including the last to himself, and deals with unbelief in the resurrection of individual believers (p. 155, above). The last chapter is devoted to an appeal for the collection on behalf of the church of Jerusalem—on which he says that he has given similar instruction to the churches

[1] This seems inconsistent with xi. 5, and it is difficult to refer that passage to ' house-churches '. There may here be an interpolation. Paul had no objection to women holding administrative offices (Rom. xvi. 1) and welcomed their activities (Rom. xvi. 6, 12). Theoretically the sexes were equal in Christ (Gal. iii. 28). Paul's remarks do not imply any readings from the Old Testament as a part of Gentile Christian worship in his time.

of Galatia (perhaps in a lost letter which was a sequel to our Galatians). He asks the individual members to set aside something for it every Sunday, and wants it completed before his arrival : then the Corinthian church is to choose delegates to carry it to Jerusalem with a letter from Paul ; or, if the sum deserve it, with Paul himself. Personal details and remarks follow : we may note that Paul states that he has exhorted Apollos to come to them, which indicates that he was not conscious of any divergence of teaching. There are greetings, including one from Aquila and Prisca (i.e. Priscilla), 'with the church that meets in their house'.

The third letter (p. 172), if, as is probable, we have a fragment of it in 2 Cor. x.–xiii., shows us Paul gravely attacked.

His changes of plan, his emphatic utterances, his conduct of the collection were challenged no less seriously than his authority to speak as an 'apostle'. The leaders of the attack were Jewish Christians from Jerusalem. At Corinth they appear to have confined their polemical activity to onslaughts on Paul's authority and character, and not, as in Galatia, to have pleaded for the acceptance of the Jewish Law by the new converts. Let them but break Paul's personal influence, and what he had planted would fall to them as ripe fruit. In spite of personal pain, Paul struck back and struck hard. Anyone who thinks himself of

Christ—and here perhaps we have a reference to the 'party of Christ' (p. 173, above)—must reckon with the fact that so is Paul : and for once Paul will not shrink from making the most of his spiritual prerogatives. Enemies must not suppose that he cannot, in personal contacts, show a force like that of his Epistles ; and he is not inferior to those who are 'superlatively Apostles' (xi. 5), even if he refused to live at the expense of the Corinthians, while accepting support from the Macedonian churches. He is thereby defeating the pretensions of the 'false apostles', who may be Satan's servants in disguise : unfortunately, the community is only too willing to tolerate them. Paul is as good a Hebrew, as good an Israelite, and his sufferings as servant of Christ exceed theirs infinitely (p. 134, above). If they talk of revelations or miracles or spiritual experiences, he can tell of being in the third heaven (p. 88, above) ; in fact, his experiences are so great that he was given some sort of physical suffering, 'an angel of Satan', in order that he might not be over-exalted : he had, therefore, thrice prayed the Lord that the 'angel' might be removed from him, and the Lord replied, 'My grace is sufficient for thee.'[1] The signs of apostolate, as shown by miracle, are in him to

[1] This story illustrates strikingly the realism with which Paul conceived of the unseen world and his relations with it.

the full, and the Corinthians are not less favoured therefore than churches founded by others. In all affection he must warn them that his impending third visit will be one of severe disciplinary measures.

Things improved, and he wrote the fourth letter of the series, 2 Cor. i.–ix., apart from the section discussed, p. 172, above.

Space forbids an analysis, but attention must be called to certain points. In this Epistle Paul sets forth his deepest reflection on the Christian ministry in its relation to those who hear its message and to those whose minds are closed, in relation again to the ministry of the Law. Suffering is of the essence of this vocation.

' Even if our outer man is destroyed, our inner man is renewed day by day . . . For we know that, if the earthly habitation in which we pitch our tent is destroyed we have a building from God, a house not made by hand, and abiding for ever in the heavens. At this time we groan, yearning to put on our heavenly habitation, since having donned it we shall not be found naked. Indeed those of us who are in the " tent " groan under affliction ; we wish not to take something off, but to put something on, in order that the mortal element may be swallowed up by life ' (iv. 16–v. 4). The gift of the Spirit is the pledge that this will be fulfilled. A little earlier Paul has said that all—all Christians, not only all

Christian ministers (who have a particular pre-
rogative of suffering and who have as their portion
the death of Jesus, in order that their converts
may have his life)—are transformed into the likeness of the Lord, from one glory into another
glory, as by the Spirit of the Lord (iii. 18).

This is a new doctrine, preparing us for Paul's
desire ' to end and to be with Christ for it is far
better ' (Phil. i. 23). The passage of the Christian
to the promised life is now seen from the standpoint of the individual ; the transformation which
had been expected as one of the concomitants of
the appearance of Christ starts now and is a
gradual continuous process ; and death is followed
not by sleep in Christ, but by union with him.
Further, the bodily existence of the present is
conceived as something burdensome and cramp-
ing. The result has definite affinities with Hellenistic personal mysticism such as had found its
way into Jewish circles. The Book of Wisdom
which Paul knew (p. 209, later) shows at times a
Greek attitude of hostility to the body and represents the soul as dwelling after death with God.

We have to remember also Paul's recent experiences, for what he says here seems to owe something to the intensity of his suffering and strain
at Ephesus. To a Semite severe illness or crushing
misfortune appeared so much like death that it
could figuratively be called death (cf. ii. 23).
Paul was undergoing something like a long-drawn-

out martyrdom ; in the speech called 4 Maccabees
(on which cf. p. 71, above), one of the heroic
brothers is thus described, ' as though in the
fire he were being transfigured into incorruption '.
As early as 1 Thess. iii. 3, Paul had thought of
suffering as necessarily falling to the lot of
Christians in general, and he had always seen
something of an antithesis between Christian
missionaries and Christian communities. We can
now observe a further individualization, which in
Philippians takes a special turn : it is an individualization in humility and not, like some Hellenistic
analogues, in self-assertion. Paul had known such
moods and resisted them.

He does not abandon the idea of Judgment or
his interest in the whole process of redemption
on the cosmic scale. Nevertheless, his thinking
shows other significant changes. The Coming is
not thought of as quite so imminent, and Paul is
no longer confident of living to see it. The New
Age which is to follow it is seen in a different
aspect. We read in Rom. xi. 32, ' God imprisoned
all men in disobedience, in order that he might
have mercy upon all men.' We must take these
words at their face value and notice the sharp
contrast with 2 Thess. iii. 2 and the advance on
Gal. iii. 22 ; the saying is announced as a *mysterion*,
a new truth revealed to Paul. The salvation of
the predestined elect was clear to him from the
beginning, but that was not all ; somehow God

would save every man. So (Col. i. 16 ff.) God would reconcile all the angelic powers to himself. In 1 Cor. xv. 24 ff. the end was victory; now it was to be a new harmony of all men, all spirits, all things. Paul had discarded the combative exclusiveness of Apocalyptic. Reconciliation is the key word of the new attitude, which brings to its climax the universalism which had been Paul's from his conversion.

At the same time, Paul modifies his former indifference to the normal values of everyday life : he speaks with respect of the Roman Empire and constituted authority (Rom. xiii.), herein reverting to the older attitude ; he allows the natural presence of goodness in the human soul (Rom. ii. 14–15) ; he gives additional counsels for the duties of family life (Col. iii. 18). Nothing is more remarkable than that in a few years Paul should have moved from the violence of 1 Thess. ii. 14 to the mellow wisdom and kindliness with which he speaks in Romans of the Jewish Law and the Jewish people. He did not allow his enemies to make him stay unreasonable.

Everything stands in a larger setting : ' For the things that are seen are of the moment, and the things that are not seen are of eternity ' (iv. 18) —not in the Platonic sense of the contrast of Ideal Forms with physical material objects, but in the eschatological meaning : the whole present world is like an elaborate back-stage decoration, which will be whisked away to reveal the final tableau that will remain. That final tableau is our dream—nay, our confident hope. Meanwhile, life has a stern earnestness, because before that tableau will be the judgment of each of us before the tribunal of Christ. The principle of conduct is the love of Christ : One died for all, so all died (that is the idea of solidarity again) : One died for all, that the living may live, not for themselves, but for him who for them died and was raised.

CHAPTER VIII

THE TRAVEL LETTERS : III. ROMANS

THE letter to the Roman church falls somewhere within the scope of the ' third missionary journey ' : it was probably written from Corinth on the happy visit which followed the correspondence, or from the port of Cenchreae. Paul has hitherto had no direct dealings with the Roman church. At the same time his faithful friends Aquila and Priscilla came from it and will have told him much of it, and quite a number of his earlier converts, in one city or another, may well have gravitated towards Rome. The Christian community in Rome seems to have come into being without any missionary act—simply as a result of the migration of men from Palestine and Syria. Suetonius says of the expulsion of Jews by Claudius from Rome (p. 129, above) : ' he banished from Rome the Jews, who were constantly in disorder on the instigation of one Chrestus ', and this has commonly been regarded as a misunderstanding of disturbances arising out of the presence of Jews and proselytes devoted to the new belief. Paul had long desired to visit this community, and then press on to Spain, in pursuit of his determination to preach on ground not broken by other missionaries, perhaps with some hope of the fulfilment of Malachi i. 11; he now hoped to do so after his carrying of the contributions of the Gentile churches to the community of Jerusalem.

The Roman church, which by 64 was numerous, was, it seems, predominantly Gentile in membership (i. 13), but with a Jewish element; the whole was Greek-speaking and had clearly been nurtured on a fairly solid diet of Old Testament knowledge. Probably, there was no single authoritative teacher and a multiplicity of smaller and larger groups and of different points of view. Certain as it is that Peter died in Rome, and likely as it is that he went to Rome from Corinth, it would seem that at the time at which this Epistle was written he had either not yet reached Rome or not yet taken a position as leader in the community.

Paul had often wished to see the community, in order to give them ' some gift of the Spirit ' (i. 11) for their strengthening. His experience had given him some insights to contribute to the enrichment of their faith in life and to the clarification of their thought. He was preparing the ground for a visit and for his Western mission. Success in that demanded a base comparable with Ephesus; Paul could not do what he wished without the support of the Roman Christians. He wrote in a most calm and conciliatory mood and obviously took more trouble over this, as a piece of writing, than over any of his other Epistles which have been preserved. In setting himself to give a reasoned exposition of his concept of the divine destiny of the Christian Church in its relation to the divine destiny of the Jewish people he made use of Wisdom; probably the only book known to him which presented a temperate and profound religious philosophy of history. He was here concerned with basic matters on which he had something of his own to say and did not discuss the resurrection ; the belief was an agreed one, detailed problems did not need to be treated except when difficulties or questions had arisen. Nor did he say anything of the Eucharist, perhaps because, as has been suggested earlier (p. 195), for him and for others this was a matter of church order rather than of theology.

The opening is studied. ' Paul a slave of Christ Jesus, called as Apostle, set apart for the Gospel of God, which he announced through his prophets in holy scriptures '—not merely the death of Christ, but the whole scheme of salvation is no new thing, but the old revelation, if that be read aright : ' concerning his Son, born of the seed of David after the flesh, appointed Son of God with power (or, by divine power) according to the Spirit of sanctification after resurrection from the dead, Jesus Christ, our Lord '—an early creedal formula, which says nothing of a pre-existence and may be (as C. H. Dodd suggests) a pre-Pauline formula known at Rome : ' through whom we received grace and apostolate to bring obedience to faith for his Name's sake among all Gentiles, among whom are you, called of Jesus Christ ; unto all those that are in Rome [1] beloved of God, called as holy : grace to you and peace from God our Father and from the Lord Jesus Christ '. Paul claims his divinely given position, but without stridency, and balances it with a statement of the divinely given position of the community of Rome.

We can only touch on certain leading ideas in the argument which follows. The Gospel is the power of God unto salvation for all believers, Jews first and (then) Gentiles. The Gospel is necessary, for without it neither Gentile nor Jew could attain righteousness. Yet neither Gentile nor Jew can plead ignorance of man's duty as an excuse for their failure to accomplish it. The Gentiles could have learned God from his works in the universe, but turned aside in folly, and worshipped idols ; their punishment was that they were allowed to sink into every kind of vice. Yet their (Jewish) critics have no reason for feeling

[1] Some MSS. omit the references to Rome here and in i. 15 and some evidence omits xv.–xvi. 24 : it has been thought that the short letter was written as a General Epistle to all Gentile churches. Cf., however, C. H. Dodd's edition, pp. xiv ff.

self-satisfied : for they too sin, and forget that God's goodness was meant to lead them to repentance and not to give them a false feeling of confidence. Further, some Gentiles can show 'the work of the Law written in their hearts' (ii. 15) —the same eternal principle of right and wrong —and the Jew who has the Law, constantly transgresses it. Circumcision and the promise to Abraham will not save him ; he has to face comparison with the obedience rendered by the uncircumcised. Yet the Jew is not without special advantages ; his nation was entrusted with 'the oracles of God', the revelation of God in the Old Testament.

All men alike are in the category of sin. The righteousness of God, attested by the Law and the Prophets, has been in Jesus revealed to all, Jew or Gentile, who believe ; they are 'justified', i.e. acquitted or saved (p. 162, above), freely through the ransoming which comes by Jesus Christ. God made him a means of atonement, and through faith we can appropriate to ourselves the benefits derivable from the Cross.

Paul uses various metaphors : justification, ransoming, purification by the expiatory value of blood, peace. They all express the belief that before Christ's coming man was alienated from God and was in a state of wrongness and inferiority ; that God had shown forbearance in the past ; that a new chapter of history had opened in which

God's righteousness, which, though it was also mercy, could not ignore sin, was fully shown forth and made available. We must not here, or elsewhere in Paul, distinguish too sharply between the abstract idea as we envisage it and the images by which it is expressed. In spite of the personal retrospect in chapter vii., the wrongness which Paul describes is not primarily a ' guilt feeling '. Rather it is a condition of which the sufferers were mostly unaware, and which could be diagnosed by a consideration of the Law (in relation to the Jews) and of conscience (in relation to the Gentiles), and healed by the use of the remedy vouchsafed to Christ. If we were considering anything of the sort, we should think of once-born men, twice-born men, heredity, inhibitions, complexes and the like. Paul, on the other hand, thought of merit, retribution, sin (for him a positive evil power), the flesh, divine Wrath, enmity, alienation, judgment and on the hopeful side of covenant, redemption, expiation ; all these concepts were vivid to him. Although at times he implies that faith opens a simple and direct way co God, he generally thinks of man's situation as involving what we should call something objectively evil : the mortgage to be paid, the bond which Christ nailed to the Cross (Col. ii. 14), the present evil age (Gal. i. 4), this body of death (Rom. vii. 24) ; and the objective remedy was Christ's self-oblation. Where Paul differs from much later thought is that he does not think of God as needing satisfaction ; God himself provides the remedy.

Man is delivered by Christ, with no reason for self-satisfaction : his merits have done nothing for him and all he shows is faith—that is to say, willingness to accept what God has vouchsafed to offer to him. To say so does not abolish the revelation of God in Scripture, since this willing faith was the characteristic quality of Abraham and was counted to him for righteousness, before he received circumcision which was the external sign or seal of his imputed righteousness. Accordingly, Abraham is the father of the uncircumcised who believe as well as of the circumcised who walk in the steps of the faith which he showed in his uncircumcised days.

Justification by faith gives righteousness and peace through Jesus Christ and the grace in which we stand and our satisfaction in the hope of God's glory, and patience, and the outpouring of God's love in our hearts through the Holy Spirit. We have nothing to fear from the Wrath ; God gave his Son for us when we were still sinners. The blessings which flow from Jesus are universal just as were the troubles which flowed from Adam— sin and death. Law multiplied sin, and sin has led to grace ; but that does not mean (as some perhaps represented Paul as saying—by a *reductio ad absurdum*) that we are to abide in sin, in order that even more grace may abound. For us sin belongs to the world of old, unhappy, far-off things which we have left. ' Or are you ignorant of the fact that all of us, who were baptized into Christ Jesus, were baptized into his death ? Accordingly we were buried with him by baptism in his death, in order that, just as Christ was raised from the dead by the glory of the Father, we too may walk in newness of life ' (vi. 3–4). This view of baptism is intimately related to Paul's conception of the Christians as the ' body of Christ ' (pp. 150, 151, above). It involves the moral inference of life with Christ : his death to sin happened once for all, but his life is a life unto God for ever : so should it be with you. Consider yourselves dead to sin and alive to God (vi. 11), and do not turn your limbs in the service of sin into weapons of unrighteousness (vi. 13). The blessing conferred on us, the new relation in which we stand to everything, heightens our moral obligation (p. 157, above). ' And now, having been freed from sin and made slaves to God, bear your fruit unto sanctification, and the end, life eternal ' (vi. 22) : you have your chance and must use it.

Paul thus states salvation in terms of his doctrine of ' being in Christ ', after stating it in terms of atonement by God's gift. He then gives a drastic picture of the struggle between the Law's demands and sin, between spirit and flesh (pp. 166–8, above). He wishes to show that such a struggle must lead to failure : that redemption by Jesus is not some sort of easy escape, but the one and only way of resolving a problem which, in the nature of things, is the same always. This new solution means having Jesus, not Law, as master, in a new marriage of the soul, and possessing his Spirit. Without it, you cannot be Christ's (viii. 9) : the Spirit is not some sort of special endowment of a pious minority : the type of life which Paul associates with its manifestations, life in the Spirit and not in the flesh (viii. 9), is for him the only type of life which belongs to the new order. To neglect it is death (viii. 13) : it is the life of sonship by adoption : and present sufferings, which are part of our identification with Christ, are as nothing compared with the glory which is to be revealed. All creation is waiting for it to be manifested : all creation has been in slavery and awaits deliverance into the freedom of the sons of God. We ourselves, though heirs, groan while awaiting (the manifestation of) our adoption, the ransoming of our body : for us hope and endurance are the marks of the present, and the Spirit aids our weakness, and groans and supplicates for us—nay, in us.

> And Sion in her anguish
> With Babylon must cope :

but our election is the great thing. ' Those whom God foreknew, he also foreordained to be shaped in the likeness of his Son, so that his Son should be the firstborn among many brethren : those whom he foreordained, he also called ; those whom he called, he also justified ; those whom he justified, he also glorified ' (viii. 29–30 : the glory is anticipatory, something to be manifested in the Day of the Lord : p. 156, above). Nothing, neither earthly suffering nor angelic powers nor anything else, will be able to separate us from the love of God in Christ Jesus (p. 155, above).

Paul ends this discussion on the triumphant note of a prose lyric, comparable with the hymn of Love in 1 Cor. xiii. He passes most abruptly to what he calls his great sorrow and unceasing pain (ix. 2), the failure of his brothers after the flesh. He could pray to be cut off himself from Christ as accursed if it would save them ; he says this most solemnly. He proceeds to suggest certain explanations for this tragic event. Physical descent is not all ; as the Scripture shows, God can dispose of men as he pleases, and creature cannot reprove Creator ; as prophecy foretold, God did in fact decide to make a new Chosen People on the basis of faith, and those whom he seems to have rejected had in fact themselves refused the mercy offered to them. While Gentiles attained righteousness by faith, the Jews had sought and not attained the Law's standard of righteousness. They had a zeal for God, but it lacked insight and they had refused to bow to the way of faith ; familiar prophecies both taught this way of faith, by implication, and foreshadowed the Jewish rejection of the Christian message. The Jews had their chance. Nevertheless, although they had rejected the offered salvation, God had not rejected the nation. Not all its members were unbelieving, and before now in the time of Elijah the faithful remnant was small. The Gentiles have no cause for self-satisfaction ; they must walk humbly before God. The secret truth is that this is a divine plan ; the majority of Israelites have erred in order that the Gentiles may be saved, and when the fullness of the Gentiles has been delivered, Israel as a whole will be redeemed. God imprisoned all in disobedience in order that he might have mercy on all. The digression ends in a brief prose hymn and we resume the argument, with a normal moral inference

So, brethren, you ought to present your bodies as a living offering to God, your worship through reason. You must be modest and harmonious, as is appropriate to the members of Christ's body (p. 151, above) : behave aright in the church, according to your various gifts,[1] in society as a whole, in the state, showing a proper submission to all legally constituted authority.[2] Live by the

[1] Cf. p. 195, above ; this looks like a self-reminiscence of 1 Corinthians. Paul, in addressing a large mixed Christian community which he had not visited, might infer its potential dangers from those which he had observed at Corinth ; but the discussion of the ' weak ' suggests that he had some specific information about internal conditions at Rome.

[2] Perhaps Paul is thinking of the riots which provoked the expulsion of Jews under Claudius (p. 129, above).

law of love, and as in face of imminent end : ' let us put off the works of darkness, and let us put on the armour of light ' (xiii. 12 : cf. pp. 210, 214, above). As a concrete illustration of the general principle, receive cordially the ' weak ', that is, those who have scruples about eating meat ; whether from genuine religious vegetarianism (such as that of the Neopythagoreans), or from Jewish scruples about clean and unclean meats and meats offered to idols, or from some special devotion (like that of James the Just) ; the weak also observed days (whether this means keeping the Sabbath, or, as seems likelier, fasting on certain days of the week). God, says Paul, has received these men : they must abstain from being censorious, but equally those who are ' strong ' ought to bear the weaknesses of the others. Each is responsible to God ; each should practise any abstinence which is necessary in view of a brother's scruples. (These men deserve consideration, whereas militant Judaizing had evoked in Paul the sharpest hostility.) May you all have harmony in the praise of God.

Paul passes to personal matters and speaks of his general mission to the Gentiles, in pursuance of which he has circled round to Illyricum.[1] At the moment, he is bearing to Jerusalem the offerings

[1] The phrase leaves it uncertain whether Paul entered the province. In any case, the reference must be to the journey which brought him to Corinth for the last time (Acts xx. 3 ; p. 134, above).

of the Gentile Christians, and hopes thereafter to pass through Rome to Spain. Meanwhile, ' I entreat you, brethren, through our Lord Jesus Christ and through the love of the Spirit, to wrestle on my behalf in your prayers before God, that I may be delivered from the unbelievers in Jerusalem, and that my ministration to Jerusalem may be acceptable to the saints, in order that I may come to you in joy and by God's will have rest with you. The God of peace be with you all. Amen.' Nothing could more clearly illustrate the justified apprehension with which Paul made this visit to Jerusalem and his awareness of the continuing tension between its Christians and himself.

At this point, the letter could appropriately end. Chapter xvi. introduces Phoebe, a woman officer of the church at Cenchreae (a harbour town of Corinth), and sends greetings to many brethren, with an incidental exhortation to avoid factionmakers and folk who serve the belly and not the Lord. The list of greetings begins with Prisca (Priscilla) and Aquila, whom we last met in Ephesus. They may have returned to Rome ; and men ' from those of Narcissus ' look like the confiscated human property of the once-powerful freedmen of Claudius, just as men ' from those of Aristobulus ' may have belonged originally to a member of the house of Herod. At first sight it may not seem likely that Paul should have so many acquaintances in a church which he had never visited, but it is possible ; many of those who had left Rome in 49 could have returned and people gravitated towards Rome. At the same time, the short exhortation (vv. 17–20), after the greetings, may seem an anticlimax, and v. 17, ' the teaching which you learned ', would be particularly natural if it was addressed to a community founded by Paul. For these and other reasons many scholars have held that chapter xvi. was a letter of introduction for Phoebe to some other church, probably that of Ephesus, which accidentally came to be attached to our Epistle. On the whole, I am inclined to believe that this chapter is addressed to Rome and that it probably was a personal letter accompanying the main Epistle, which is in the nature of a treatise ; G. La Piana has made the very attractive suggestion that it was directed to a group of Paul's personal friends in the city. One new piece of evidence has just come to light. A papyrus in the Library of the University of Michigan, coming from the famous find of which the larger part is in the Chester Beatty Collection and datable as not much, if at all, after A.D. 200, places the doxology xvi. 25–27 at the end of chapter xv. This heightens the probability that xvi. 1–24 is an independent composition. While the doxology is open to serious doubt, no one questions the Pauline authorship of vv. 1–24.

CHAPTER IX

LETTERS OF THE CAPTIVITY

COLOSSIANS, Philemon, and Philippians were all written from prison. Where was this prison ? Till recently Rome or Caesarea were the only claimants ; but of late various scholars have suggested that one or all came from Ephesus. The question is important, since the hypothesis of Ephesus puts all these letters earlier than had been thought (some would place Philippians as coming even before 1 Corinthians) and would invalidate some of the views usually held on Pauline development. The reader will find a full statement of the case for the Ephesian captivity in G. S. Duncan's book, *St Paul's Ephesian Ministry*, and a reply in C. H. Dodd's lecture, *The Mind of Paul. Change and Development*. For my own part, I hold that it is just thinkable that Colossians and Philemon (which bears in itself no characteristic marks save its linking to Colossians) were written at Ephesus, but I see no reason to doubt that Philippians was written from Rome, and I prefer to ascribe all three to Rome.

If new evidence should ever appear to confirm the Ephesian hypothesis, it would make some difference in our general view of the evolution of Paul's ideas. The line 1 Thessalonians—1 Corinthians—2 Corinthians i.–ix.—Romans would still show to us the gradual waning of the immediacy of the Second Coming in Paul's mind, the change to a universal hope for men (whereas the reconciliation of angelic powers in Colossians would not represent a later stage ; Rom. viii. 21 had pointed this way), and the development of an individualization in the hope of immortality (p. 204, above). At the same time we should have to place somewhat earlier the formulation of an advanced Christology in Philippians and Colossians (and here too the issue is only one of elaboration).

Philippians may well be the latest of the three, but it is convenient to treat it first. Paul wrote this Epistle after making his defence (i. 7), under the shadow of an impending decision, which would be life or death. Nevertheless, the note of the letter is one of joy and trust—trust in God and in the community ; Paul is not troubled about the decision. He would fain die and be with Christ, ' for that is far better ', but at the same time continuance in the flesh would serve the needs of his disciples, and that possibility of service was far more important to him than any personal preference. He was wholly free from the egotistic passion for martyrdom which sometimes appeared.

At the moment, he expresses confidence that he will be able to rejoin his friends at Philippi (i. 25–6,

ii. 24). But he might die, and that death would in some sense have a sacrificial value ; ' even if I am poured out as a libation on the sacrifice and service of your faith ' (ii. 17). The idea of martyrdom as something possessing value and merit transferable to others had assumed importance in the time of the Maccabee revolt. We have already seen Paul's view of suffering ; it gained a new emphasis. Meanwhile, his mind was devoted to the practical service of the Gospel. He has, he says, already had considerable and successful activity as a teacher in the place of his imprisonment. All is not ideal ; some are preaching Christianity from unworthy motives and wish to add to his distress, but in any case, Christ is preached, and Paul does not here have to complain of false teaching.

Paul is thanking the men of Philippi for a gift which they have sent by Epaphroditus. He writes in simple gratitude and affection : ' Paul and Timothy, slaves of Christ Jesus ' : in addressing these beloved brethren he does not need to stress his apostolicity. After a particularly warm expression of gratitude to God for his every recollection of them, and praying that their love may wax yet warmer, he describes his present situation. To die and be with Christ were far better : the only point of living is the need of the churches. They too encounter opposition and have had the privilege of suffering for Christ. He exhorts them to live worthily and harmoniously, and thereby to fill his cup of joy. ' Have this thought in your life together which you have as members of Christ Jesus, who being in the form of God, did not regard equality with God as a piece of luck, but laid aside his dignity, taking the form of a slave, being born in the likeness of men, and being found in shape as a man humbled himself, being submissive even unto death, and that death on a cross. Wherefore God exalted him exceedingly, and gave him a Name above every name (i.e. the name of *Kyrios*, " Lord "), that in the Name of Jesus every knee of heavenly and earthly and subterranean beings should bow, and every tongue should acknowledge that Jesus Christ is Lord to the glory of God the Father ' (ii. 5–11).

We have seen earlier the inevitable exaltation of Jesus as Lord (p. 78, above). The fact that the exalted Jesus, in the interval between his Crucifixion and his Second Coming, could not be thought of as inactive, was perhaps the reason why activity was ascribed to him as a pre-existent divine force, and why he was identified with various divine virtues of the type postulated by later Jewish literature, Wisdom and (as in John) the Logos or Word-Reason of God (a term avoided by Paul). A closer elaboration of thought along these lines is characteristic of the later Pauline writings : it is equally characteristic of Paul that here, as in 2 Cor. viii. 9, an ethical inference is drawn from Christ's self-humbling in assuming our nature in order that we may

become ' in Christ '. The language is solemn as
the thought, and perhaps reproduces an earlier
formulation.

One other aspect of this Epistle demands com-
ment. At the beginning of chapter iii. we pass
abruptly from personal matters and good wishes
to a warning against dogs, evil workers, Judaizers.
This has been regarded as a fragment from another
Epistle, and iii. 1 to iv. 23 may come from an earlier
letter thanking the Philippians for their gift. Nevertheless, a larger measure of structural looseness
can be allowed in this intimate Epistle than in
earlier and controversial works. Accordingly, the
question is an open one ; it is just possible that
iii. 2–14 is almost a quotation from a previous letter
of Paul to the Philippians ; this could be so if iii. 1,
' to write the same things ', refers forwards and not
backwards. The issue itself can have been raised at
the time of the Epistle as a whole, since we learn
from i. 15–18 that Paul's foes had not abandoned
their struggle against him.[1] False teachers were
perhaps not the only thing that troubled Paul ; those
' whose God is their belly ' (iii. 18 ; cf. Rom. xvi. 18)
may be simply bad Christians.

---

[1] Some had argued that the enemies in question are
not Judaizing Christians, but Jewish teachers. The
difference was perhaps not so clearly marked as we
should think : but the will to carry on propaganda is
clearly attested for the Judaizers. Still, the matter must
be left open.

Philippians shows Paul in a most warm-hearted and attractive aspect. So does the letter which we shall handle next.

The Epistle to Philemon is a brief personal note from Paul (and Timothy) to a rich citizen of Colossae (just possibly of Laodicea), Philemon, and Apphia and Archippus and the church in Philemon's house. Paul, who is here simply 'a prisoner of Christ Jesus', begins with the thankfulness he expresses to God every time he thinks of Philemon. He has a request to make. A slave called Onesimus had run away from Philemon and come under the influence of Paul's teaching. Paul was faithful to his principles (p. 205, above) and sent Onesimus back, at the same time tactfully hinting that he would have liked to keep him as a helper, but he would do nothing without Philemon's approval. Paul pleads for humane treatment, delicately, but with a clear implication that the fulfilment of his wishes is a matter of loyalty, and writes in his own hand to say that he will pay for anything that is due (probably Onesimus, in running away, had carried off money of Philemon's). At the same time, he asks Philemon to prepare a guest chamber for himself, for he hopes to be at freedom thanks to the prayers of the faithful. The preservation of this note in spite of its personal and ephemeral character, is a testimony to the zeal with which Pauline matter was preserved by those who made the collection.

The Epistle to the Colossians, Philemon's community, was addressed to a community which Paul had never visited although its founder, Epaphras, was probably a disciple of his and had come to Paul, apparently in some anxiety about the well-being of the church. Paul, ' an apostle of Christ Jesus through the will of God ', and Timothy, are the senders. After the usual complimentary thanksgiving, he says how, since he heard from them, he has been constantly praying for them that they may be filled with the knowledge of the will of God, who has ransomed them from the power of darkness and transferred them to the kingdom of the Son of his love, in whom we have redemption and remission of sins. That is to say, the Christians are already citizens of the Messianic Kingdom. The functions of Christ are then described in accordance with the later Pauline development (p. 224) and in language which is elaborated rather than spontaneous. Christ is the image of the unseen God, the firstborn of all creation, because in (or, by) him were created all things, visible and invisible —angelic powers of every order. Christ was the means and end of the whole activity of creation and the means also of the whole (parallel) activity of redemption. He was pre-existent, all exists in him, and he is the head of his body, the Church.

In the last point—and in the reference which follows to Christ as the means of reconciliation and to the peace made through the blood of his Cross —we see ideas which are a normal part of the Pauline view of election and redemption. But what comes before is not a necessary inference from this ; rather, it is the application to the Messiah, as a supernatural being, of Hellenistic Jewish notions of the functional powers of God. Jesus the teacher, having become the Lord Christ, drew to himself elements from the metaphysical structure which had been built up between God and phenomena. The cosmic statement in this passage of Colossians may have been largely the product of meditation on the Hebrew text of Gen. i. 1, interpreted in the light of Prov. viii. 22.

Just as in Philippians, Paul draws a moral lesson ; Christ did thus in order that he might set you holy and blameless and without reproach before himself (at the Judgment), if you remain grounded in faith and do not swerve from the hope of the Gospel which you have heard and which has now at last been proclaimed in all creation under heaven, ' of which I, Paul, became a minister '. Just as you received Jesus Christ the Lord, so walk in him. Do not be led astray by ' philosophy and vain deceit, in accordance with the tradition of men '.

There was such a source of error at Colossae. Unfortunately for us, Paul did not need to say precisely what it was, since the Colossians knew it better than he did. We have to infer its nature from allusive references and also from the positive teaching set forth as a corrective. Paul begins by stressing the complete sufficiency of Christ and Christ's final defeat of angelic powers. From this and from other points we learn that the heresy involved attached importance to other supernatural powers. Further, there was a strong element of legalism : ' So let no one judge you in eating and drinking or on account of a feast or new moons or Sabbath ; all these things are a shadow of the destined future ; but the body is that of Christ.' Paul proceeds to speak of a worship of angels and of men depending on visions, puffed up by the mind of their flesh, and practising asceticism.

The arguments used by Paul are parallel to those of Galatians ; angelic powers and regulations about food and days belong to the old superseded way of living. But the situation was something different. At Colossae Paul's apostolical authority was not at stake and the movement which troubled him was something altogether more impersonal and abstract. It is not clear that circumcision was urged. Further, there was clearly an emphasis on intermediary powers, ' angels ', and there was ' disregard of the body '. These are phenomena which can be associated with forms of heretical Judaism. The reader should be reminded that while the main body of Jewish opinion was probably akin to the classic Judaism of the second century and later, there were in various places tendencies to approximate to the ideas of paganism and to form occasionally new and esoteric beliefs. We have seen the way in which

Paul brought elements from orthodox Judaism with him on his conversion. Jews of a different type would bring other elements and their contribution is one of the factors which went to produce the tendencies of thought and piety which are commonly grouped under the name of Gnosticism.

The Christology of this Epistle is elaborated in a document called in our New Testament ' To the Ephesians '. The address is certainly not original : for in the greeting the words ' in Ephesus ' are omitted by some of our best textual authorities, and Ignatius, who knew the document and who habitually in writing to communities refers to Apostolic letters, makes no mention of it in his letter to the Ephesians. The writer of the Letter addressed himself to Christians in general, ' to the saints who are faithful in Christ Jesus '. He can hardly have been Paul, but what he gives is mainly a Pauline mosaic, and may involve a use of lost Pauline Epistles in addition to those which we know. The argument elaborates the high doctrine of Colossians, without having any such immediate reference to actual danger. The style differs from that of Paul : not to mention points of detail, it has a sustained serenity which is quite unlike his way of writing. That could possibly be explained as due to the handiwork of some assistant, employed in the way in which Josephus employed them, or to necessary elaboration of an unfinished posthumous work—although neither explanation would account for the absence of Paul's inspired irrelevances and violent transitions. But can we escape the implications of iii. 4–5, ' in the mystery of Christ, which in other generations was not revealed to the sons of men, as it has now been revealed to his holy apostles and prophets in the Spirit ' (cf. ii. 20) ? That is the language of the sub-Apostolic period.[1]

The shadow of wrong teaching does not fall across this picture : if the wrong teaching attacked in Colossians was such as we have supposed, and if Ephesians belongs to the next generation of Christians, this kind of wrong teaching had ceased to be a problem. Otherwise, Ephesians adheres closely to the pattern of Colossians, adding a further elaboration of the doctrine of the Church.

There remain the Epistle to the Hebrews, which, though in the papyrus codex mentioned earlier, makes no explicit claims to be by Paul, and is later and different, and the group of what are called the Pastoral Epistles—the two to Timothy and the one to Titus. In style and vocabulary the Pastorals differ widely from the undisputed Epistles, and they belong to a wholly other world of Christian life and thought. The Church is an organized society,

---

[1] The suggestion that the writer of Ephesians was the man who made a collection of Paul's letters and that (as Goodspeed urges) he meant it as an introduction to them deserves attention. That the writer was not Paul seems to me certain ; but a considerable body of critical opinion takes the other view.

which has long been such : ' faith ' is not an eager turning to Christ as the means whereby the individual can share a corporate salvation, but the acceptance of a tradition divinely imparted to the Apostles, *or* simply that tradition. The readers are warned against contemporary errors, in general terms which lack all the concrete vigour of Paul's attacks on ideas which seemed to him erroneous : to have been more specific would have involved glaring anachronisms. Genuine fragments of Pauline letters are perhaps incorporated, but the hypothesis involves great difficulties. These writings in their present shape are an early illustration of the tendency which in the fourth century produced the *Constitutions of the Apostles*, a comprehensive manual of Christian practice. Ephesians, though not by Paul, is Pauline ; the Pastorals as a whole are not.

CHAPTER X

THE STYLE AND THOUGHT OF PAUL

A BOOK of the end of the second century known as the *Acts of Paul and Thecla* describes the Apostle as ' small in stature, baldheaded, bowlegged, of vigorous physique, with meeting eyebrows and a slightly hooked nose, full of grace '. This calls up a vivid picture ; but we have no reason to believe it to be true and we must be content to know Paul from his writings.

We have all been taught that the style is the man. Style in self-conscious authors, indeed, is not so much the man himself as the man in the part which he wishes to play, or to be thought to play, upon the stage of life. Less sophisticated writers, as for instance the authors of the first two Synoptic Gospels, do not assume poses. Paul is much more akin to them than to the self-conscious type : not because he was in any sense deficient either in the art of writing or in the desire to persuade and move his readers, but because of the extreme earnestness and simplicity with which his themes absorbed his attention and because of his fatherly love for his converts and eager anxiety to help them. He is anything but artless ; he concludes often his discussion of a topic with a rounded and effective close, and he can attain the heights of prose, as for instance in 1 Cor. xiii. and Rom. viii. 31–9 ; but as we study these passages we cannot but feel that their elevation comes entirely from within. Paul clearly has a well-developed sense for rhythm, and uses effective parallelism and other forms of ornament, but he does not think of himself as a writer ; he expressly disavows any such pretension (1 Cor. ii. 1 ; 2 Cor. xi. 6).

His independence of the art of rhetoric as it was understood in his time is shown by his failure to organize the subject-matter of his letters in a methodical structure. He has his own scheme of an Epistle, which is related to the ordinary scheme of the letter as then written ; but within that scheme he passes from subject to subject, with an unrestrained use of vigorous parentheses. His style with its homely, if occasionally artificial, illustrations and metaphors has one contemporary pagan counterpart, the diatribe. This was a type of popular philosophical causerie which had been crystallized as a literary form by Bion the Cynic in the third century before Christ. Like the Pauline Epistles, it was full of rhetorical questions, often brief and in rapid succession, of short imaginary dialogues, and of small illustrative anecdotes. The essential similarity lies in the fact that the diatribe, like the Epistles, was intended to produce the effect of a spoken style; both have the same loose vigour. We cannot prove that Paul had not read works of the diatribe type, though we shall see reason to form a very limited idea of his use of books, but in any case, he could be thoroughly familiar with this mode of discourse from what he heard. Cynic philosophers talked at street corners to any and all who would listen, and Paul must have heard them at times; and much of what they said would be reasonably congenial, for the Cynics attacked popular vices, and popular superstitions.

Paul's Greek is a noteworthy phenomenon. It is not literary, but at the same time it is not like the careless Greek of the popular letters which have survived on papyrus; although it resembles them in its freedom from many of the grammatical canons of the schools, it has not their helplessness and verbosity. There are no formal periods, and indeed the art of using the period was a declining one, but there is a rhetorical movement and energy which express a powerful personality that did not shrink from coining bold phrases such as Gal. ii. 7, ' the Gospel of circumcision '.

A single strong influence, that of the Greek Old Testament, runs through this style. I am not speaking of direct quotations. These are rare except in the long argumentative letters to Corinth, Galatia and Rome, where they serve deliberate ends : to reinforce Paul's own position against his adversaries by an appeal to the authority which they stressed so strongly; and (as is clearly true of Romans, which is above controversy, and is true in a measure of the others) to represent what had happened as something which, in God's eternal plan, had to happen and therefore must necessarily have a happy ending (Rom. xv. 4). The striking phenomenon is, rather, that there is not a paragraph in Paul's writings which does not include subconscious recollections of the Greek Old Testament just as every paragraph of *Pilgrim's Progress* echoes the King James Bible. Greek writers frequently quoted Homer and Plato, and sometimes used Homeric phrases as a literary device ; but such recollections are on an infinitely smaller scale. Paul shows only the slightest acquaintance with pagan Greek literature, but he knew his Old Testament very well.

A great classical scholar, Eduard Norden, has remarked, ' Paul is a writer whom I, at least, understand only with very great difficulty.' Probably all classical scholars would agree. The reason is that Paul's style is full of second-hand Semitisms which come from the Greek Bible. Paul must have had some acquaintance with the Old Testament in Hebrew also and seems to see some of the original connotations which underlie the Greek as he quotes it ; but the Greek version is the fact of importance.

This stylistic phenomenon corresponds to a fact of the greatest importance in the whole writing and thought of Paul and in the whole development of early Christianity. The expression is externally Hellenic, but inwardly Jewish. The proportion of born Jews within the Christian movement diminished steadily, but at the same time the Jewish scriptures remained the scriptures of the new movement before and after they had created their own supplementary scriptures, and the development of Christian thought in the century succeeding Paul's death is inextricably bound up with the history of Christian attitudes towards the Old Testament. This is the more remarkable when we reflect that the Septuagint was a bulky and expensive book, which would correspond in cost to the *Encyclopaedia Britannica* rather than to the Bible to-day. Further, it was a book which a Greek convert would have great difficulty in reading unless he had been prepared for it. In fact, the acquaintance of the community at large with the Old Testament seems probably to have turned on sermons and on the existence of anthologies of prophetic testimonies to the coming and nature of Christ. They represent the literary product of that movement of exegetical theology which we have seen beginning in the very earliest days of the life of the Church of Jerusalem.

It is well to contrast Paul with a Jew of the

preceding generation, Philo. For Philo, as for Paul, the Old Testament is the supreme revelation not only of God's will for every man, but also of all the wisdom after which man was thereafter to strive. But Philo's interest in the Old Testament was principally in the Pentateuch : he makes some quotations from the prophetic books, but he is not primarily concerned with them, since he was mainly interested in the Law, which by implication contained all that man needed to know of himself and of God, and had very little interest in the possibility of the sudden establishment of a new order on earth. Further, while Philo quotes the Old Testament constantly as the ultimate authority, his style is not saturated with reminiscences of it, but is the normal philosophic Greek of the period. Philo retained the Law, which Paul rejected : but, whereas Paul interpreted it with reference to what he held to be the novel facts of the situation, Philo showed the Hellenism, which he had side by side with his essential Judaism, by relating the Law to general concepts and to psychological and metaphysical abstractions.

The second generation of Gentile Christians were more thoroughly trained than the first in Jewish tradition. Although the language and cere- monies of Christianity could not fail to acquire connotations from the general thought and beliefs of the Gentile world which used similar language and comparable rites, still the otherness remained

(p. 182, above), and the Christians were a 'third people', so called as being distinct from both Gentiles and Jews.

The thought of Paul is such as his style indicates. He makes no attempt to harmonize concepts which may seem logically inconsistent. He never says 'probably' or 'possibly'; the only shading of language which he employs is his occasional distinction between the instructions and teaching which he gives as coming from the Lord and those which he gives as of his own authority; and he clearly expects his disciples, in fact, to follow both equally. Once more we may contrast Philo. Philo's writings give an abundance of suggestions on everything which was not already determined by the Law in a manner which was too definite to be surmounted by exegetic subtlety. Philo is a speculative thinker, Paul an authoritative teacher. Philo shows an intense interest in contemporary and earlier Greek philosophic thought, and follows pagan thinkers very freely when their doctrines were not wholly irreconcilable with Jewish tradition; Paul uses an occasional concept (e.g. in Romans, the idea of conscience and the belief that the Gentiles had the Law written in their hearts, which looks like elementary Stoicism, but can at the same time be a recollection of Jer. xxxi. 33); but that is all, and the authority of human teachers is nothing to him. He says: 'For me to live is

Christ Jesus ' ; he could have equally said : ' For me to think is Christ Jesus.' He refers the problems, even the small problems, which arise to that revaluation of all things which he had made in the light of his scheme of thought. Jesus had died and risen ; this death and rising had given to those who could and would by faith secure them the blessings of a new relation with God ; this relation could be described as justification or salvation, and it was mediated by dying with Christ and rising with him in baptism and it was both expressed and made possible in the gift of the Spirit ; it involved a quasi-physical union with Christ and union with other believers, not in virtue of a common humanity, but in virtue of a common being in Christ ; it made both possible and obligatory conduct according to a new way of life which was binding as the Law had been, but which unlike the Law could through the new gift of the Spirit and a new union with Christ be observed by men.

Once more the contrast with Hellenic Judaism is highly instructive. For Philo and his like, the central issue turns on man as an individual, who by the aid of God and thanks to God's powers in the world and God's willingness to accept repentance, must strive to realize the full stature of which man was capable. This stature was the expression of the soul as a thing essentially immortal. Philo was not concerned with the question of the indefinite survival of human personality, but with the possession by man as man of a spiritual element which was qualitatively immortal. Paul represents the older, un-Hellenized Jewish view which was preoccupied with the nation and not with the individual. It was the old hope of Israel, not the immortality of the soul. He says in Romans that all creation groans and travails up to this time, and the new order which is to come involves a reconstitution of all things. The present universe was to Philo a revelation of God, to Paul at best indifferent. For Paul there would be a new heaven and a new earth, and the salvation of the elect individual was part of the salvation of the Elect as a whole. Paul says with passionate sincerity that he would be willing to lose his own salvation if only his people, the Jewish people, could at that price be saved. This statement would have been entirely unintelligible to Philo.

Paul naturally picked up some of the philosophical, possibly a little of the religious, terminology of the time, much as a man to-day does not need any special knowledge to acquire the words ' evolution ' and ' relativity '. Paul shows no closer understanding of paganism ; he generally views it in terms of the condemnation customary in Jewish apologetic literature. Herein Philo, though more urbane, differs less, for the reason that not merely did he as a Jew reject pagan worship as idolatry, but also he followed philosophic traditions in which popular cultus was usually represented at worst as a vulgar superstition and at best something which must be maintained because of civic associations. Paul met at Corinth one feature of Gentile belief, the tendency to suppose that a rite was a thing in itself which operated without reference to the moral value of the initiate's subsequent conduct. This, like the hostility which Paul encountered from Judaizers, was to Paul simply one of the works of the flesh ; even the best of paganism, its quest for wisdom, was but another snare (p. 175, above).

In conclusion we must briefly consider the old question of the relation of the teaching of Paul to the teaching of Jesus. The antithesis is patent and has often been so treated as to represent Paul as the man who spoiled a simple and beautiful Gospel by the arbitrary introduction of quarrelsome subtleties. This is a shallow view, but there is a real question. What does Paul mean when he says, ' Even if we have known Christ after the flesh, we know him so now no more ' (2 Cor. v. 16) ? And why does he so seldom quote actual sayings of Jesus ? The problem is the more pressing, since not only was there a considerable body of ethical and other sayings of Jesus in oral circulation at the time (as the sayings of Jewish teachers were regularly preserved), but also Paul himself shows a certain amount of subconscious recollection of extant sayings of Jesus. Why does he not quote them more often in writing to his converts?

He quotes sayings of Jesus with reference to eschatology (p. 154, above) and marriage (p. 179, above), and he quotes them, just as he recalls the words spoken at the Last Supper, as sayings which possess a binding authority. He may well have quoted more sayings in his oral teaching; the Epistles are supplementary instruction on issues which arose when he was absent. On many of these it would not have been possible to quote Jesus; so, for instance, on the problem of the Law, to which Jesus had maintained an attitude of loyalty though claiming the right to interpret it, on the problem of Gentile converts, on meats offered to idols (though we could imagine a use of Matt. xv. 17 ff.), on spiritual gifts, on the internal discipline of a Christian community and its relation to other Christian communities. Nevertheless, there is a further point. For Paul the earthly life of Jesus, however noble, is an incident in the existence of the Lord and is more-over of that order of events which preceded the Crucifixion and Resurrection. Since, as the opening of Romans says, Jesus was appointed the Son of God with power, a new world order has been initiated; its fruition will not be seen fully until the day of the Lord, but already in those who believe and who belong to Christ, it is the order of the world. The central figure under God of this new order, or rather the figure who will remain central until his work is done, is the Risen Lord, who himself, or by, or in, or as the Spirit, determines and guides in matters large and small the life of the community which is his body in the world. For Paul this guidance was objective exactly as was the memory at Jerusalem of what Jesus had said.

Paul only thrice commends the imitation of Christ: in 1 Thess. i. 6, where the virtue to be copied is that of suffering in joy, in Rom. xv. 7, 'receive one another as Christ received you', and in Col. iii. 13, 'even as Christ forgave you, so also do ye' (where the reference is to the Risen Lord and not to the Jesus of history); in 1 Cor. xi. 1 Paul exhorts his converts to imitate himself, as he, Paul, imitated Christ. Elsewhere Paul alludes to the voluntary poverty of Christ (2 Cor. viii. 9), that is, as in Phil. ii., to his laying aside his princely state; and in Rom. xv. 3 he expresses the same meaning by saying that Christ 'pleased not himself'. Normal Christian life, however, was not a matter of imitating Jesus, but was life by the Spirit in Christ.

The primitive Apostolic preaching was concerned with the death and resurrection of Jesus, with the fulfilment of prophecy in them and in the outpouring of the Spirit on the community, and with the expectation of the second Coming.

The sayings of Jesus were valued from the earliest times of the movement, but their setting in the narrative framework or written Gospels was the product of an historical interest which arose at a time when the Church was an institution which had already a generation of corporate life behind it, and when the original disciples who had lived and eaten with Jesus had mostly died or grown old, and the expectation of a second coming was on the wane. Under changed conditions it was necessary not only to supply the answers to some of the questions which piety asked, but also to reinforce that piety in daily life when it was no longer lived in the first intensity. Further, the experience of Paul had shown that the free life of the Spirit had its dangers in communities which had not a background of Jewish ethical training. Paul had been compelled to formulate the rudiments of a Christian ethic ; the sub-apostolic period demanded more concrete direction.

However we formulate the relation of Paul's writings to the sayings of Jesus, we must never forget that in some of the weightiest matters Paul understood and developed ideas of Jesus which were obscured and imperilled at Jerusalem. Freedom in face of the Law, a generous outward-turned view of humanity, a zeal to save men at the cost of correctness—these were the marks of both Jesus and Paul. Neither tolerated

All the easy speeches
That comfort cruel men.

Much of what Paul said became unintelligible, much unnecessary, to a later age. His doctrine of the Spirit had to be modified at a time when the instruction not to quench the Spirit seemed a good deal less important than the necessity of distinguishing between spirits. His concept of the body of Christ was an incidental metaphor and not a central idea as the Church became more and more a human institution in which people grew up. His opposition to the Law was replaced by the interpretation of the Old Testament, or the moral code thereof, which he himself began. The issue between Gentile Christianity and Judaistic Christianity ceased to be a living issue when Judaistic Christianity was a very small minority and in fact broken by the siege of Jerusalem and the accompanying dispersion. The new unity was created in which Peter and Paul could be thought the joint founders of the Roman Church, and the letters of Paul passed from being utterances of the moment to become authoritative documents themselves needing exegesis. On the face of it Paul in his lifetime had sustained many bitter defeats and the type of Christianity which prevailed seems to bear many of the features which he had opposed; nevertheless, although without Paul Christianity had reached Gentiles and would have reached more Gentiles, it is Paul more than any other man who was responsible for the fact that Christianity was not a Jewish sect but an independent body with an independent life.

BIBLIOGRAPHY

THE reader should supplement his use of the Revised Version by turning to J. Moffatt, *The New Testament. A new translation* (1913, etc.). The same writer's *An Introduction to the Literature of the New Testament* (3rd ed., 1918, and reprints) is an invaluable guide ; for other points of view see M. Dibelius, *A Fresh Approach to the New Testament and Early Christian Literature* (1936), E. J. Goodspeed, *An Introduction to the New Testament* (Chicago, 1937), and A. Jülicher—E. Fascher, *Einleitung in das Neue Testament* (7th ed., Tübingen, 1931 ; the 2nd ed. was translated by J. P. Ward, 1904).

Of the innumerable commentaries we may mention : in English, those of W. Sanday and A. C. Headlam, and C. H. Dodd on Romans, E. deW. Burton on Galatians and J. E. Frame on Thessalonians ; in French, M. J. Lagrange on Galatians and on Romans ; in German, H. Lietzmann, *Handbuch zum Neuen Testament* (Tübingen, various editions ; in collaboration with Dibelius, Windisch, and others ; brilliant and penetrating), H. L. Strack—P. Billerbeck, *Kommentar zum Neuen Testament aus Talmud und Midrasch* (Munich, 1922–8 ; invaluable for Jewish material), and the exhaustive re-editions of H. A. W. Meyer's *Kritisch-exegetischer Kommentar über das Neue Testament* (by various hands ; very full). G. Kittel, *Theologisches Wörterbuch zum Neuen Testament* (Stuttgart, 1932 ; with many collaborators) performs the function of an admirable commentary on very much in

BIBLIOGRAPHY

Paul. P. N. Harrison, *The Problem of the Pastoral Epistles* (1921) is a very able study.

For the general evolution of early Christianity see H. Lietzmann, *Geschichte der Alten Kirche*, vol. I—(Berlin, 1932; the first two volumes have been translated by B. L. Woolf, as *The Beginnings of the Christian Church*, 1937–8); A. von Harnack, *Die Mission und Ausbreitung des Christentums* (2 vols.: ed. 4, Leipzig, 1924; 2nd ed. translated by J. Moffatt as *Mission and Expansion of Christianity*); MacKinley Helm, *After Pentecost* (New York, 1936); S. J. Case, *The Evolution of Early Christianity* (Chicago, 1914); M. S. Enslin, *Christian Beginnings* (1938).

A. Schweitzer, *Paul and his Interpreters* (translated by W. Montgomery, 1912), surveys much of the history of Pauline exegesis and foreshadows the interpretation given in his very striking *The Mysticism of Paul the Apostle* (translated by W. Montgomery, 1931). Two lectures by C. H. Dodd, *The Mind of Paul : a Psychological Approach* (Bulletin of the John Rylands Library, XVII, 1933, pp. 3–17), and *The Mind of Paul : Change and Development* (*ibid.* XVIII, 1934, pp. 3–44), are illuminating. E. Schwartz, *Charakterköpfe aus der antiken Literatur*, II, pp. 97–125, is brilliant and should be translated. The earlier period of Paul's life is acutely discussed by W. L. Knox, *St. Paul and the Church of Jerusalem* (1925), as is the later period in his *St. Paul and the Church of the Gentiles* (1939); his Schweich Lectures for 1942, *Some Hellenistic Elements in Primitive Christianity* (1944) are important. For the evidence of Acts, cf. F. J. F. Jackson—K. Lake, *The Beginnings of Christianity* (1920–33 ; includes valuable material by H. J. Cadbury and others). On the later part of Paul's life G. S. Duncan gives a new hypothesis in *St. Paul's Ephesian Ministry : a reconstruction with special reference to the Ephesian origin of the Imprisonment Epistles* (1929). Note also K. Lake, *The Early Epistles of St. Paul* (1911

BIBLIOGRAPHY

and later); M. S. Enslin, *The Ethics of Paul* (1930); W. H. P. Hatch, *The Pauline Idea of Faith in its relation to Jewish and Hellenistic Religion* (Cambridge, Mass., 1917; he and Cadbury contributed two good essays to *Studies in Early Christianity edited by S. J. Case, presented to F. C. Porter and B. W. Bacon*, New York, 1928); R. Bultmann's article *Paulus* in Gunkel-Zscharnack, *Die Religion in Geschichte und Gegenwart* (ed. 2).

For the geographical background, see the writings of Sir William Ramsay, specially *St. Paul the Traveller and the Roman Citizen* (1895 and later), and A. Deissmann, *Paulus. Eine kultur-und religionsgeschichtliche Skizze* (ed. 2, Tübingen, 1925; translated by W. E. Wilson, 1926, as *Paul : a Study in Social and Religious History*). For the historical and cultural background, see above all M. Rostovtzeff's classic works, *The Social and Economic History of the Roman Empire* (1926), *The Social and Economic History of the Hellenistic World* (1941), and *The Cambridge Ancient History*, vols. X–XI. For the Jewish background, see the comparable work of G. F. Moore, *Judaism in the first centuries of the Christian Era. The age of the Tannaim* (Cambridge, Mass., 1927–30). For the pagan religious background, see F. Cumont's equally magnificent *Les religions orientales dans le paganisme romain* (ed. 4, Paris, 1929; 2nd ed. translated by G. Showerman); A. Deissmann, *Light from the Ancient East* (translated by L. R. M. Strachan, ed. 4, 1927); W. R. Halliday, *The Pagan Background of Early Christianity* (Liverpool, 1925); A.-J. Festugière—P. Fabre, *Le monde gréco-romain au temps de Notre Seigneur* (Paris, 1935; cheap and excellent); A. D. Nock, *Early Gentile Christianity and its Hellenistic Background* (in *Essays on the Trinity and the Incarnation*, ed. A. E. J. Rawlinson, 1928), and *Conversion* (1933).

INDEX

INDEX

INDEX